# The Children Act Guidance and Regulations

## Volume 9

## Adoption Issues

A NEW FRAMEWORK FOR THE CARE
AND UPBRINGING OF CHILDREN

LONDON: HMSO

First published 1991
ISBN 0 11 321474 X

Printed in the United Kingdom for HMSO
Dd295242 10/91 C280 G3392 10170

# Preface

This volume is number nine in a series produced in the context of the Children Act 1989 and issued under section 7 of the Local Authority Social Services Act 1970. Its contents are as follows:

Chapter 1: Children Act 1989: Changes to Adoption Law

Chapter 2: Adoption Allowance Regulations 1991: Guidance

Chapter 3: Adoption Contact Register and information about birth records.

Local authorities will need to review their existing policies and practice in the light of the Regulations and guidance and give the same priority to these responsibilities as to other statutory duties.

For a proper understanding of other relevant guidance and regulations, this volume should be read in conjunction with other volumes in this series.

Regulations associated with the guidance on adoption allowances are contained in Annex A to this volume.

# Contents

# CHAPTER 1    CHILDREN ACT 1989: CHANGES TO ADOPTION LAW

1.1. The Children Act 1989 has led to a number of amendments to adoption legislation. Most of these amendments are to be found in Schedule 10 of the Act; some important repeals of the Adoption Act 1976 are found in Schedule 15.

1.2. The changes can be grouped as follows:

(i) amendments consequential upon changes in concepts and terminology introduced by the Children Act;

(ii) amendments designed to harmonise adoption law across the jurisdiction of England and Wales, Scotland and Northern Ireland;

(iii) a small number of substantive changes designed to remedy particular defects in adoption law or to introduce improvements for which an opportunity had been awaited.

## CONSEQUENTIAL CHANGES

### a. 'Parental responsibility' – formerly 'parental rights'

1.3. The courts have come to regard parental responsibility as a collection of powers and duties which follow from being a parent and bringing up a child, rather than as rights which may be enforced at law.

1.4. Parental responsibility is defined to include all the rights, powers, authority and duties of parents in relation to a child and his property [section 3(1)]. The value of the term 'parental responsibility' is twofold. First, it unifies the many references in legislation to parental rights, powers and the rest. Secondly, it more accurately reflects that the true nature of most parental rights is of limited powers to carry out parental duties.

### b. 'Looked after by a local authority' – formerly 'children subject to a care order or in voluntary care'

1.5. A child is looked after by a local authority if he is in their care or provided with accommodation by the authority in the exercise of their social services functions [section 22(1)].

1.6. The Children Act makes a clearer distinction between the voluntary and compulsory powers of local authorities. The status of 'voluntary care' is abolished along with the power to assume parental rights by an administrative resolution. Compulsory powers may only be obtained by court order and even then parents retain parental responsibility.

A local authority's duty to make plans for children whom they look after is strengthened; the involvement of parents and others in decision making is required and after-care functions are also given new emphasis.

### c. Emergency Protection Order

1.7. One of the new orders created by the Act is an emergency protection order. Among the powers which were repealed by the Act is section 34 of the Adoption Act 1976 which gave a local authority the power to remove a protected child from unsuitable surroundings to a place of safety.

1.8. This order enabled a child to be removed for up to 28 days with no right of appeal or challenge. Additionally, the powers and duties of the person who obtained the order were uncertain. These aspects have been justifiably criticised and the Children Act tries to find a better balance between the need to protect children and the other interests of the individuals involved.

1.9. The introduction of an emergency protection order is intended to provide one set of criteria and powers for removing a child to a place of safety when he might otherwise suffer harm. The conditions which must be satisfied before an emergency protection order may be made are closely linked to the purpose of the order. Parents and others are given a right of challenge; the duration of the order is shorter than the place of safety order and the legal effect of the order is more clearly spelt out.

1.10. The court is no longer able to make a care order if it refuses to make an adoption order but it may direct a local authority to make enquiries to decide whether to bring court proceedings. This approach accords with the Children Act's aim of establishing a single set of criteria for care orders.

### d. Family proceedings

1.11. The term 'family proceedings' is important for two reasons. Firstly, the court has full order-making powers in such proceedings and, secondly, the rules which permit separate proceedings to be consolidated come into play. Adoption proceedings now become family proceedings under the Children Act. Courts hearing adoption applications have powers to make section 8 orders on application or of their own volition.

1.12. The present power of the court to make adoption orders with conditions avoids possible alarm that greater "openness" and availability of access provides no protection to the parties involved.

'Family proceedings' are the key to the Act's flexibility.

### e. Other orders made by the court

1.13. By the repeal of sections 14(3) and 15(4) of the 1976 Act, courts are no longer required not to make an adoption order in favour of a step-parent if the court considered a divorce court custody order would be preferable. By the repeal of paragraphs (1), (3) and (4) of section 37 of the 1976 Act, courts are no longer required to consider whether custodianship – replaced by residence orders – would be better. Courts are also now free to make a residence order whether or not parents have agreed to adoption.

1.14. These measures accord with the Children Act's intention of giving the courts a free hand to make whatever orders best serve the interests of the child. They also simplify a complex set of provisions of the Act.

## Harmonisation of UK Adoption Law

### Main provisions

1.15. The Children Act presented an opportunity to harmonise certain aspects of adoption law within the United Kingdom and Northern Ireland. The main improvements included:

(i) approved adoption societies in Scotland and Northern Ireland are able to operate in England and Wales;

(ii) children who are 'protected children' under the law in Scotland and Northern Ireland are also protected in England and Wales;

(iii) courts in England and Wales are able to order the return of a child who has been removed in defiance of adoption law in Scotland and Northern Ireland;

(iv) the provision of counselling services in connection with applications from adopted people for information about their birth records is to be made available in Scotland and Northern Ireland for people whose adoption took place in England or Wales;

1.16. Where necessary, these legislative provisions were reciprocated by similar amendments to Scottish law. Reciprocation in Northern Ireland will be effected by new legislation in due course.

# SUBSTANTIVE IMPROVEMENTS AND INTRODUCTIONS

## a. Protected children

1.17. Amendment to section 32 of the 1976 Act brings the protected status of a child to an end if no adoption order is made within two years from the giving of the notice. Such an amendment is necessary because under the old law it was possible for a child to be a protected child until he reached the age of 18 years if applicants (usually the step-parents) applied for an adoption order and subsequently allowed the application to lapse without formally withdrawing it.

## b. Freeing for adoption

1.18. Children are no longer treated as being 'in the voluntary care' of a local authority. The Children Act makes provision for arrangements to be made for a child to be accommodated by a local authority or on their behalf. Such arrangements can be terminated at any time. Similarly, a child is no longer, 'in the care of' a voluntary organisation. The measures are designed in part to enable parents to have confidence in the voluntary nature of 'accommodation'.

1.19. These changes have lead to a corresponding restriction of the right to apply to free a child for adoption. Under the old law, an application could be made without the consent of a parent or guardian if the child was 'in the care of' an adoption agency. This phrase was not defined in the 1976 Act but was taken to include a child in voluntary care. In future, however, an adoption agency will not be able to apply for a freeing order without the consent of a parent or guardian unless the agency is a local authority in whose care the child is by virtue of a care order.

## c. Step-parent and spouse

1.20. Section 14 of the Adoption Act 1976 has been amended to allow a step-parent and a spouse who is the natural parent of the child to apply for an adoption order where the natural parent of the child is at least eighteen years of age and the step-parent at least twenty one. Previously, both the natural and step-parent had to be at least twenty-one.

## d. Adoption Contact Register

1.21. The Children Act provides for the Registrar General to operate an Adoption Contact Register. The Register enables adopted people and their birth parents and other relatives to be put in touch with each other [Schedule 10, paragraph 21 of the Act inserts a new section 51A into the Adoption Act 1976]. This Register builds upon the informal contact service which the Registrar General has operated in recent years.

1.22. The Register will only be open to peole who are at least eighteen years of age. The Registrar General will pass on to the adopted person who has registered with him the name and address of a relative who has asked for his details to be placed on the Register. In order to use the Register, the people concerned will have to satisfy the Registrar of their identity and, in the case of the relative, of their relationship with the adopted person. A fee will be charged.

## e. Disclosure of birth records of adopted children

1.23. A further amendment to the 1976 Act extends the arrangements to enable people to obtain information about their birth records. A person who was adopted before 12 November 1975 is required to attend a counselling interview before he may be given infromation about his birth records [Adoption Act 1976, section 51]. A person adopted after 11 November 1975 is not required to attend a counselling interview but such services should be made available to him.

1.24. The amendments permit counselling to take place in the United Kingdom or from a body outside the United Kingdom which has notified the Registrar General that it is willing to provide counselling and satisfies the Registrar that it is suitable to do so.

1.25. A series of 5 booklets have been produced jointly by the Office of Population Censuses and Surveys and the Department of Health concerning the Adoption Contact Register, obtaining access to birth records and providing advice to counsellors.

Annex B to this volume reproduces these booklets for ease of reference.

### f. Adoption Allowances

1.26. In future, new adoption allowances, paid to adopters and those who intend to adopt, will no longer be paid under individual schemes approved by the Secretary of State. Such payments will now be subject to Regulations and Chapter 2 of this volume contains guidance on the application of these Regulations.

# CHAPTER **2**    **THE ADOPTION ALLOWANCE REGULATIONS 1991: GUIDANCE**

2.1. The Adoption Allowance Regulations 1991* come into force on 14 October 1991 under the Children Act 1989. The Regulations replace adoption agency schemes for the payment of adoption allowances under section 57(4) of the Adoption Act 1976. These schemes are revoked from 14 October 1991. From the same date, subsections 57(4) to (10) of the Adoption Act 1976 are revoked and section 57A is introduced (reproduced at Annex A).

2.2. From 14 October 1991, adoption agencies have to consider, assess and pay all new adoption allowances in accordance with the Regulations and provide information about allowances under the Regulations to adopters who are already receiving an allowance under a revoked scheme. It will no longer be required for local authorities to submit adoption allowance schemes to the Secretary of State for approval or amendment. The Regulations will enable any adoption agency (whether a local authority or an approved society) to pay an adoption allowance subject to the provisions in the Regulations. The Regulations set parameters within which agencies will be required to consider eligibility and assess payment. Adoption allowances continue to be the exception rather than the norm. However, like the schemes which they replace, the Regulations are intended to give agencies sufficient flexibility to respond to individual needs and circumstances within this overall objective.

2.3. Under Regulations an approved adoption society which does not hold itself out as being an agency which normally pays allowances, unlike local authorities, is under no obligation to decide whether or not to pay an allowance, but it is not prevented from doing so in a particular, exceptional case. If it does consider paying an allowance in a particular case it will need to follow certain procedural obligations (see paragraphs 2.15 to 2.18 below).

2.4. The Regulations enable adopters who were already receiving an allowance before commencement to choose between continuing to receive the allowance under the conditions which applied in a revoked scheme or to receive instead an allowance under the Regulations. The same choice is available to adopters where an allowance becomes payable which was agreed in principle, subject to the satisfaction of particular conditions specified in a revoked scheme.

2.5. However, families who obtained a court order to adopt a child before 14 October 1991 and who did not qualify for an adoption allowance under the previous scheme at the time the adoption was being arranged will not be able to apply for an adoption allowance under these Regulations.

2.6. The Regulations reflect the principles which led to the introduction of adoption allowance schemes in 1982. The central principle is still that an adoption allowance may be payable to help secure a suitable adoption where a child cannot be readily adopted because of a financial obstacle. The Regulations also draw upon the experience of adoption agencies and central Departments in the operation of allowance schemes in the years since 1982, as schemes have developed to take account of new or changing circumstances.

---

* known as 'the Regulations' throughout this Guidance.

2.7. Finally, the Regulations draw upon the research of the National Children's Bureau who were commissioned by the Department of Health and Welsh Office to monitor the operation of adoption allowance schemes (*Adoption Allowances in England and Wales: The Early Years', HMSO, 1988*). This research firmly demonstrated the importance of adoption allowances in facilitating the adoption for children who would otherwise be unlikely to have the opportunity for permanance and security which adoption provides.

## THE REGULATIONS: SUMMARY

2.8. The Adoption Allowance Regulations 1991 exercise the powers conferred by section 9, paragraphs (2) and (3) and also section 57A of the Adoption Act 1976 which was introduced on 14 October 1991 by virture of paragraph 25, Schedule 10 to the Children Act 1989. The Regulations enable adoption agencies to pay allowances to people who intend to adopt a child in pursuance of arrangements made by the agencies. Adoption agencies may also pay allowances to people who have already adopted a child, where an allowance was agreed or paid under an approved scheme.

2.9. The Regulations set out the circumstances in which an allowance may be paid (Regulation 2), factors governing the amount of the allowance (Regulation 3), the procedure to be followed in determining whether an allowance may be paid (Regulation 4), information to be supplied about an allowance (Regulation 5), the procedure for review, variation and termination of an allowance (Regulation 6) and confidentiality, preservation and access to records (Regulation 7).

## DEFINITIONS

2.10. Regulation 1 defines terms which appear throughout the Regulations, including the following:

'Adopters' may be a married couple or one person in accordance with sections 14 and 15 of the Adoption Act 1976; the term includes prospective adopters, in which case the question of whether an allowance is payable must be decided before the adoption order is made. It also includes adopters who have already adopted a child and who receive an allowance under a revoked scheme, or in respect of whom an adoption allowance was agreed in principle before the adoption order was made on the basis that a particular circumstance, related to the child's needs, emerged at a later date.

2.11. 'Adoption agency' applies to a local authority or to an adoption society approved by the Secretary of State under section 3 of the Adoption Act 1976. The 'agency' referred to throughout the Regulations applies to the agency with responsibility as principal for placing the child for adoption, notwithstanding that another agency may be included in the arrangements. This agency makes the relevant decision under Regulation 11(1) of the Adoption Agencies Regulations 1983 to place the child for adoption and has responsibility for considering, determining and paying any adoption allowance. In practice, where interagency arrangements are operating, the responsible agency will usually be a local authority.

2.12. 'Adoption panel' applies to a panel established in accordance with Regulation 5 of the Adoption Agencies Regulations 1983. For the purpose of these Regulations, the term applies to the panel of the principal adoption agency whose functions are defined in the preceding paragraph.

2.13. Agencies should note that the term "allowance" is intended to apply to a periodic or regular payment payable at intervals to be determined by the agency. Where a single lump sum or capital payment is required in connection with the child's circumstances – for example, in order to purchase special equipment or to make adaptations to the home – local authorities can assist by exercising powers available in other legislation. This applies whether an allowance is to be paid by the authority or by another adoption agency (or, of course, whether or not an allowance is paid at all). Such legislation includes the Chronically Sick and Disabled Persons Act 1970 and powers which are available in Part III of the Children Act 1989 in relation to children in need.

## CIRCUMSTANCES IN WHICH AN ALLOWANCE MAY BE PAID

2.14. In order to determine whether an adoption is, or is not, practicable unless an allowance is paid, the agency will need to consider all the child's circumstances in relation to those of the adopters, with particular reference to Regulations 2 and 3 in each case.

## PROCEDURE FOR DETERMINING PAYMENT OF AN ALLOWANCE – SUMMARY

2.15. The starting point for agencies to consider paying an adoption allowance is Regulation 4. Regulation 4(1) sets out the procedure for determining whether an allowance should be paid in accordance with paragraphs (1) and (2) of Regulation 2, concerned with the circumstances in which an allowance may be paid.

**Unless one of the specific exemptions apply, agencies will need to have completed the procedure set out in Regulation 4 before the adoption order is made.**

2.16. Two things need to have happened before a decision can be made as to whether the general circumstances of Regulation 2(1) have been satisfied.

The adoption panel will need to have made a recommendation –

(i) whether this particular adoption by these particular adopters would be in the best interests of this particular child, and

(ii) whether this adoption is practicable without payment of an adoption allowance.

The adoption agency then has to make a decision on those recommendations. Only if the agency decides that the proposed adoption is in the child's best interests and that the adoption would not be practicable without payment of an allowance will they be able to decide that the adopters are eligible to receive an allowance.

2.17. However, since all the circumstances set out in Regulation 2 (1) and (2) must be satisfied before an adoption allowance is payable, the agency making the arrangements will need to know that at least one of the circumstances listed in Regulation 2(2) is satisfied before referring the matter to the adoption panel.

More detailed guidance on the procedure for determining whether an adoption allowance should be paid is contained in paragraphs 2.60 to 2.69 below.

2.18. The agency which is "making arrangements" for the child's adoption is the agency with responsibility for placing the child for adoption. It is common in interagency practice for a second agency to make a decision, after considering the recommendation of its adoption panel, that a prospective adoptor is suitable to be an adoptive parent. Where that decision is conveyed to the placing agency, it is the placing agency which is responsible for deciding, after considering the recommendation of its own panel, whether a prospective adoptor would be a suitable adoptive parent for a particular child. This decision is made in accordance with Regulation 11(1) of the Adoption Agencies Regulations 1983.

2.19. Specific circumstances are set out in Regulation 2(2) in which an allowance may fall for consideration. The specific circumstances are as follows:

## i. Established Relationship

2.20. Regulation 2(2)(a) provides for an allowance to be considered where, before placement for adoption, the child has established a strong and important relationship with the adopters. This situation will apply where a child has been living with foster parents who wish to adopt him but who cannot afford to lose the fostering allowance which they have been receiving in respect of the child. An adoption allowance will not, or course, apply automatically to former foster placements. The adopters' financial circumstances in relation to the child's needs must be assessed in the same way as all placements. In some cases, an adoption allowance will not be payable, where, after assessment, the agency determines that the adopters are able to afford the additional cost of caring for the child as a permanent member of the family. Where foster parents are not willing to undertake the parental responsibility of maintaining the child without an allowance being paid, although able to do so, adoption may not be appropriate.

2.21. The agency will be expected to have a good understanding of the foster placement in order to evaluate the relationship between the child and his foster parents. The regular evaluation and monitoring of all foster placements, required under the Foster Placement (Children) Regulations 1991 and the Review of Childrens' Cases Regulations 1991, will be of assistance to the agency in forming a judgement about such a placement. These two statutory instruments are reproduced in Annex B and F respectively of Volume 3: 'Family Placements'.

2.22. Where the agency considers that the child should be placed for adoption with his foster parents, it is important that the agency is satisfied that the distinction between the two types of placements is understood by all parties, including the child. The date on which the fostering placement ends and the adoption placement begins should be notified to the adopters under Regulation 12(1) of the Adoption Agencies Regulations 1983. Where an adoption allowance is payable, it is recommended that payment should commence from the date of the adoption placement. This will enable the agency to evaluate the adoption placement in the circumstances which will apply after the adoption order is made and will assist in the preparation of the Schedule 2 report in connection with the adoption hearing. The date on which the fostering allowance ends and the adoption allowance, where appropriate, begins should be notified to the adopters in writing as part of the notification required under Regulation 5.

2.23. In common with all prospective adopters, foster parents who become prospective adopters are entitled to apply for Child Benefit from the date of placement for adoption. They should be advised to apply. In most cases, the level of adoption allowance will be lower than the former fostering allowance because Child Benefit will be deducted from the amount of adoption allowance which would otherwise be payable. The only circumstance in which Child Benefit should not be deducted is where the adopters are receiving Income Support (see Regulation 3).

2.24. Adoption allowances cannot include the 'reward element' (professional (foster care) fees) which maybe payable to foster parents as part of a fostering allowance in recognition of the service which the foster parent provides to a local authority in caring for a child who is the responsibility of the authority. An adoption allowance will therefore always be lower than a former fostering allowance in which a 'reward element' was included.

## ii. Siblings and other children

2.25. Regulation 2(2)(b) provides for payment of an allowance where it is in the child's best interests to be placed for adoption with siblings; or in order to join siblings in an adoptive placement; or where a child may have shared a home with an unrelated child with whom he has developed close ties.

## iii. Special Needs

2.26. Regulation 2(2)(c) applies where, at the time of placement for adoption, the child is identified as being mentally or physically disabled or suffering from the effects of emotional or behavioural difficulties (or a combination of these conditions), and as a result of the condition the child requires a special degree of care which necessitates extra expenditure.

2.27. The expression "mentally or physically disabled" in Regulation 2(2)(c) is not restrictively defined and is intended to include children who are sensorily impaired. Children who show emotional or behavioural difficulties may include those who have experienced physical or sexual abuse, or both.

2.28. In all cases to which Regulation 2 applies, the role of the Medical Adviser to the Adoption Panel will be of special value in evaluating the degree of the child's condition and in providing advice to the agency who will in turn notify the adoptive parents. The Medical Adviser would be expected to seek specialist medical advice where appropriate.

2.29. Payment of the allowance is intended where the child's condition is serious and long-term. For example, where a child needs a special diet or where items such as shoes, clothing or bedding need to be replaced at a higher rate than would normally be the case with a child of similar age who was unaffected by the particular condition. Again, the child may need to be closely supervised for his own safety or for the protection of others. Specialist assistance may be needed – for example, regular attendance at a nursery, possibly with special ancilliary assistance, or visits to a clinic or consultations with a paediatrician, which may result in unforeseen expenses for the adopter.

## iv. Payment in principle

2.30. Regulation 2(2)(d) applies where, at the time of placement, the child is mentally or physically disabled or had emotional or behavioural difficulties but payment of an allowance is not immediately justified because the child's condition had not yet reached the stage where extra expenditure is required. However, the nature of the child's condition is such that there is a risk of deterioration which could result in higher than average expenditure for the adopters at some future date. To guard against this risk, therefore, the agency may agree in principle to the payment of an allowance and at some future date effect the payment if they are satisfied that the child's condition has deteriorated to make the payment of an allowance necessary and that the adopters' financial circumstances merit this.

2.31. Regulation 2(2)(e) applies where at the time of placement, it is known that the child carries a high risk of developing a medical condition, the nature of which would result in higher expenses for the adopters, if the condition were to develop, than was the case at the time the child was placed for adoption. This circumstance would apply, for example, where information relating to the child's medical or genetic history was such that there existed strong grounds for concern about the child's medical prognosis.

2.32. It will often be evident to the agency that an allowance may be needed in respect of the child's specific circumstances before prospective adopters are found. Where, after considering the recommendation of its panel, the agency considers that an allowance may become payable in principle because of the child's circumstances, it should include this information in its written report about the child under Regulation 7(2)(e) of the Adoption Agencies Regulations 1983. It will be helpful to the agency's social workers charged with the task of finding suitable adopters (or to any second agency involved in finding a family) to know that payment of an allowance may be considered, subject, of course, to the circumstance of the prospective adopter.

2.33. Where, after receiving the recommendation of its panel, the agency subsequently decides under Regulation 11 of the Adoption Agencies Regulations that adoption by the particular adopters is in the child's best interests, the agency will need to apply Regulations 3 and 4 to the adopter's circumstances in relation to those of the child in order to decide whether an adoption allowance is needed in respect of the particular placement.

2.34. The child's need for permanence and security should always be the prime consideration in the selection of adopters. However, entitlement to an allowance does not automatically follow if the child's circumstances satisfy one or more of the conditions specified in the Regulations. There may be occasions where, after the agency has decided that an allowance may be payable in principle, payment of the allowance cannot be justified after taking account of the adopter's circumstances and the child's needs under Regulation 3 where the agency conclude that the adopters are able financially to take on the added responsibility of caring for the child. Some prospective adopters may prefer to assume, unaided, the whole responsibility for meeting the child's needs and feel able to do so.

## ADOPTIVE PARENTS IN RECEIPT OF THE ADOPTION ALLOWANCE UNDER A REVOKED SCHEME

2.35. Regulation 2(3) enables the agency to pay an allowance in accordance with the Regulations to:

(a) adopters who, before the Regulations came into force on 14 October 1991, were receiving an allowance under a scheme which has been revoked and who agree to receive an allowance complying with the Regulations, or

(b) adopters is respect of whom the agency had agreed that an allowance would be payable subject to the satisfaction of any particular condition. This would apply, for example, where the agency had agreed in principle to pay an allowance subject to a deterioration in the child's health.

2.36. All the adopters referred to in this Regulation should be given information about receiving an allowance in accordance with the Regulations instead of under the terms and conditions which applied to a revoked scheme. Adopters who received payment for a revoked scheme can receive an allowance in accordance with Regulations only if they agree to this. Adopters who do not wish to receive an allowance under the Regulations are entitled to continue to receive an allowance under the terms and conditions which applied to a revoked scheme.

## INFORMATION TO ADOPTERS

2.37. Regulation 2(3) should be read in conjunction with Regulation 4(2)(a) and (b). All allowances which are in payment on 14 October 1991 should continue to be paid in accordance with terms and conditions set out in a revoked scheme. However, as soon as reasonably practicable after 14 October 1991, agencies should contact all adopters who are:

(i) receiving a payment under a revoked scheme; or

(ii) in respect of whom payment under a revoked scheme had been agreed in principle subject to particular conditions being satisfied or subject to an adoption order being made.

2.38. The agency should inform such adopters about the terms and conditions which apply to allowances made under the Regulations including information to show how such allowances are determined. The information should include an indication of the amount of any allowance which the adopters would receive under the Regulations. This may, of course, be the same as their existing allowance. Particular care should be taken to ensure that adopters are made aware of any benefits or disadvantages which may arise from a transfer to the Regulations. Adopters may find it helpful to discuss the position in person with a social worker. Adopters should not, of course, be expected or encouraged to agree to an allowance under the Regulations where this may result in arrangements which may be less favourable than those which applied under a revoked scheme. Adopters who are receiving an allowance, or for whom an allowance has been agreed, in respect of a child whose circumstances differ from those in Regulation 2(2), may also receive an allowance under the Regulations if they wish. It is not necessary for the agency to review its orginal decision to pay an allowance.

2.39. The agency is only required to determine an allowance under the Regulations, including the amount of any allowance, if the adopters who are receiving payment under a revoked scheme agree to receive an allowance after they have had an opportunity to consider the information about the Regulations which has already been supplied to them. Where the adopters do not wish or agree to receive an allowance under the Regulations, the agency should continue to pay an allowance as determined under the former scheme.

## CHANGES OF CIRCUMSTANCE

2.40. Regulation 2(4) sets out conditions relating to changes of circumstance. These conditions must be agreed by the adopters before an allowance is payable. The adopters should be notified of these conditions as part of the written notification about adoption allowances required under Regulation 5.

2.41. The adopters are required to inform the agency immediately if:

(i)   the child ceases to have his home with the adopters, ie, if the child's departure from the family home is regarded by the adopters as a permanent departure. Temporary absences – for example, for respite care, hospitalisation or attendance at a boarding school – do not apply because the child's permanent residence remains with the adopters' family; or

(ii)  the family move, so that the agency can continue to issue payments to the correct address and also because there may be a need to reassess the level of allowance; or

(iii) the child dies.

2.42. Regulation 2(4) also requires the adopters to notify the agency immediately of any significant change in their financial circumstances or in the child's financial needs or resources.

2.43. The agency will need to operate with sensitivity in determining how far changes in financial circumstances or needs affect the allowance payable. It may, for example, be inappropriate to offset cost of living earnings increases against the adoption allowance although marked increases may be taken into consideration. Similarly, any marked deterioration in the child's condition leading to extra expenditure for the adopters may justify an increased allowance following reassessment.

2.44. Similar considerations apply when the allowance is reviewed annually. Regulation 2(4)(b) specifies that before the allowance is payable, the adopters should agree to complete and supply to the agency an annual statement of their financial circumstances and the child's financial circumstances, including financial needs.

## DATE OF PLACEMENT

2.45. Regulation 2(5) is concerned with the date of placement for adoption. Where all the conditions specified in the Regulations have been satisfied and the agency has decided that an allowance should be paid, the agency and the adopters should clearly understand and agree the date from which the payment is to commence. The adopters must be notified in writing of the date payment is to begin, the amount and how it is to be paid.

2.46. As in the case of former foster placements it is recommended that the adoption allowance should commence from the date of placement for adoption. Payment of an allowance is not conditional upon an adoption order being made. Payment at the time of placement will help to underline the significance of the relationship between the child and adopters. It will also assist the agency to evaluate the relationship in the circumstances which will exist after the adoption order is made and provide an opportunity for the agency to judge, at an early stage, whether any adjustments need to be made to the initial amount of the allowance. The adopters are entitled to Child Benefit from the date of placement and should be advised to apply.

2.47. Where an agreement is made in principle to pay an allowance after the adoption order is made, ie because the conditions specified in Regulation 2(d) or 2(e) are satisfied, the adopters and the agency must understand and agree that the allowance will only be payable in respect of the child's needs. For example, an allowance will not become payable because of a change relating to the adopters' circumstances which is unrelated to the child's condition, such as the loss of a job.

2.48. Similarly, a change in the circumstances of the child which could not have been predicted at the time the agency agreed in principle to make a payment could not automatically initiate payment of an allowance unless the criteria in Regulation 2(2)(d) or (e) are fulfilled.

2.49. An adoption allowance may only commence after an adoption order has been made where the circumstances in Regulation 2(2)(d), (e) or 3 apply.

## ASSESSING AMOUNT OF ALLOWANCE

2.50. Regulation 3 sets out the factors to be taken into account by the agency in determining the amount of allowance payable. The Regulations set broad parameters within which an assessment should be made. However, the amount of allowance payable in individual cases is a matter for the agency to determine, taking account of the child's needs and resources and the adopters' circumstances. Assessment of the various factors calls for careful and sensitive judgement. In assessing the amount of allowance the aim is to facilitate a successful placement and to enhance the child's well-being in the adoptive home. In undertaking its assessment, especially before the adoption placement, the agency will need to project forward and consider all the financial circumstances which are likely to apply when the child is living in the adoptive home.

2.51. Specific factors to be taken into account, and set out in Regulation 3(2), are:

(a) financial resources available to the adopters;

(b) the amount needed by the adopters; and

(c) the financial needs and resources of the child.

### (a) Financial Resources available to Adopters

2.52. The assessment of any adoption allowance must take account of the financial resources available to the adopters, including any financial benefit which would be available in respect of the child after adoption. Factors will also include any projected earnings available to the adopters. Significant income from capital investments may also be taken into account. However, the value of the adopters' home should not be included. Any known financial benefit – such as social security benefits – which the child will bring to the adoptive home, will also be considered. However, in accordance with Regulation 3(3), any mobility or attendance allowance* which the child receives (or subsequently becomes entitled to) should not be included as a source of income. In common with most revoked adoption allowance

---

* These allowances will be replaced by a new disability living allowance from April 1992.

schemes, the Regulations provide for mobility and attendance allowance to be disregarded.

2.53. Where an adoption allowance is payable, the adopters are entitled to claim Child Benefit from the date of placement for adoption. Child Benefit should be taken fully into account in determining the financial resources available except where the adopters are receiving income support, when Child Benefit is taken fully into account in the income support assessment. In such a case, the agency should disregard Child Benefit until the adopters cease to receive income support.

## (b) Amount needed by Adopters

2.54. The amount needed by the adopters in respect of their reasonable outgoings and commitments (excluding outgoings in respect of the child) needs to be assessed. The assessment should take into consideration expenses and outgoings which are familiar and accepted items of family expenditure. The aim of the assessment is to assist the agency to determine the additional cost to the adopters of caring for the child. Factors for consideration will include housing and daily living expenses, transport costs, expenses related to children who are already part of the adoptive home, family outings and holidays. Adopters should be encouraged to give as many details as possible in respect of their outgoings. The adoption should not result in financial hardship or lead to a situation in which the success of the placement is jeopardised because of financial embarrassment.

## (c) Financial Needs and Resources of the Child

2.55. The financial needs and resources for the child should also be taken into account. The agency should consider all factors, including everyday financial needs, as well as any special needs and expenses related to the child's individual circumstances. Examples of special needs (though these are by no means exhaustive) would include special diet, replacement bedding and clothing resulting from heavy usage, transport costs associated with medical treatment or transport costs to school, not otherwise available from the local education authority.

2.56. Occasionally, there will be circumstances in which the child has his own financial resources other than social security benefits payable in respect of him. This might, for example, include income arising from a capital investment or trust fund and would be considered by the agency as part of its assessment.

2.57. Agencies will have to exercise care and sensitivity in having regard to the standard of living of the family which the child is to join and which he will, of course, be expected to share. It is fair that such differences should be recognised, within reason, but obviously it is not the intention of the adoption allowance provisions to subsidise what might be considered a very high standard of living.

2.58. Regulation 3(4)(a) specifies that the amount of allowance payable must not include any element of remuneration for the care of the child by the adopters. There should be no element of reward or profit payable to the adopters. The allowance should be governed by costs arising from any additional needs related to the child's circumstances. It has come to light that some allowance paid under approved schemes have included some element of remuneration, although no approved scheme included such a provision. This practice must cease.

2.59. The amount of the allowance should not exceed the amount of the fostering allowance (excluding any element of remuneration to the adopters) which would have been payable if the child were fostered by the adopters. This is specified in Regulation 3(4)(b). In determining the amount, the agency should have regard to variations in the level of its fostering allowances in relation to the child's age. Enhanced allowances, payable solely in respect of the child, which would be payable if the child were fostered, should form part of the agency's consideration. Similar criteria should apply between fostering and adoption allowances in respect of such enhancements. For example, where a child's needs are such that he would qualify for a specific rate of enhanced fostering allowance payable by the agency if he were fostered, the same enhanced rate should be payable in the adoption allowance. The only exception to comparable enhancements is in relation to fostering allowance enhancements for special occasions such as Christmas and birthdays. Since the child will cease to be the responsibility of the agency on adoption, such enhancements should not be included in the adoption allowance.

## PROCEDURES FOR DETERMINING WHETHER AN ALLOWANCE SHOULD BE PAID

2.60. Regulation 4 sets out the procedure which the agency should follow in order to determine whether an allowance is payable in an individual case. The determination will result in the agency's decision under Regulation 2(1)(b)(ii) whether the adoption is, or is not, practicable without payment of an allowance.

2.61. An approved adoption society will not usually be obliged to follow the procedure for deciding whether to pay an adoption allowance – see paragraph 2.3 above. Regulation 4(3) makes clear that an approved adoption society which does not hold itself out as an allowance paying society shall not be required to comply with sub-paragraphs (a) and (b) of paragraph (1), concerning whether an allowance may be paid and supplying information to adopters, and need comply with sub-paragraphs (c), (d) and (e) of paragraph (1) only if they have considered whether or not to pay an allowance to adopters.

The following paragraphs 2.62 to 2.69 deal mainly with the procedure to be followed by adoption agencies which are to determine whether an allowance will be paid.

2.62. Regulation 4(2)(b) ensures that adopters whom an agency had decided was entitled to payment under a revoked scheme remains entitled under the Regulations, ie Regulation 4(2)(b)(i) exempts the agency from considering whether an allowance is payable under Regulation 4(1)(a). Adopters who had not received a payment under a scheme before 14 October 1991 can only receive a payment calculated in accordance with the Regulations.

2.63. When the agency makes the decision that adoption is in the child's best interests it is recommended that, at the same time, the agency should consider whether the child's circumstances are such that an allowance may become payable on placement. These circumstances are set out in Regulation 2(2). The advice of the adoption panel will be especially valuable in helping the agency to identify whether an allowance may be needed in order to facilitate the child's adoption. Such considerations are particularly important at this stage if it is thought necessary to seek placement with an adoptive family from another agency.

2.64. When the agency subsequently decides to place the child with particular adopters, the adopters should be advised that an allowance may be payable after the agency has considered the adopter's circumstances in relation to those of the child. The adopters should be given advice and information about the principles underlying adoption allowances, as well as information about the items in Regulation 3 relating to the calculation of an allowance and the arrangements in Regulation 6 with regard to review, variation and termination of allowances. It is recommended that the adopters should be given this information as part of the agency's written proposals in respect of the adoption under Regulation 12(1) of the Adoption Agencies Regulations 1983. The agency should ensure that further advice and information which may be required with regard to the allowance is made available to the adopters.

2.65. Unless the adopters do not wish to receive an allowance, the agency should assess the circumstances of the adopters and the child in accordance with Regulation 3. The agency should notify the adopters in writing of its proposed decision about whether any allowance is payable, and if so, the proposed amount. The notification to the adopters should specify the period of time during which the adopter may consider the agency's proposals and make any representations to the agency. Regulations do not specify the period of time allowed. However, this should provide sufficient opportunity for the adoptors to consider carefully the agency's proposals whilst not unduly prolonging the date of placement. A period of 28 days from the time the proposed decision was sent to the applicants is suggested as a guide to good practice.

2.66. In this context, the attention of local authorities is drawn to the Complaints Procedure Directions 1990. Voluntary adoption societies should be operating their own complaints procedures as a matter of good practice in connection with their responsibilities as adoption agencies. It is especially important that such procedures should be in place where a voluntary adoption society is considering payment of an adoption allowance in respect of a placement which it is arranging. Adopters should be given an opportunity to ensure that all the circumstances relating to the proposed placement have been taken into account by the adoption agency.

2.67. After considering any representations the agency should reach its final decision with regard to the allowance and notify the adopters in writing setting out the information specified in Regulation 5.

2.68. It is not necessary for the agency to reach a decision about the amount of allowance payable in cases where, in accordance with Regulation 2(d) and (e), payment of an allowance is subject to developments related to the child's condition which may occur after placement. In such cases, however, the agency should ensure that adopters are aware before placement of the conditions subject to any allowance which will subsequently be made, including how the allowance will be assessed and arrangements for review, variation and termination (see paragraphs 2.72 to 2.79 below). Such adopters should be advised to contact the agency in the event of any deterioration in the child's circumstances to enable the agency to determine whether an allowance is subsequently payable in accordance with Regulations 3 and 4. The adopters will also need to understand before placement that any allowance will only become payable in respect of the child's needs.

2.69. An approved adoption society is only required to provide information about allowances to adopters and to follow the requirements in Regulations 3 and 4, where that society is considering paying an allowance in respect of a child which the society is placing for adoption. Where, as is common in inter-agency practice, an approved adoption society has decided, on the recommendation of its adoption panel, that prospective adopter is suitable to be an adoptive parent, and where the decision has been conveyed to the adoption panel of the placing agency, it is the placing agency which is required to decide whether an allowance is payable in respect of the particular placement after receiving the recommendation of its own adoption panel.

# NOTIFICATIONS ABOUT ADOPTION ALLOWANCES TO ADOPTERS

2.70. Regulation 5 sets out the information about the allowance which the agency must provide to the adopters after the agency has made a decision to pay an allowance in an individual case. The information must be given in writing and should confirm information which was supplied to the adopters whilst the agency was reaching its decision. It is for agencies to determine their own arrangements for payment. However, agencies may find it convenient to pay adoption allowances using similar arrangements to those which apply to payment of fostering allowances, including a common date for annual review. Calculation of allowances should project forward, anticipating circumstances which are likely to prevail in the year ahead as far as practicable.

2.71. The information to be included is as follows:

(a) the method by which the adoption allowance has been determined;

(b) the amount of allowance to be paid to the adopters;

(c) the date on which the first payment will be made;

(d) the method by which the allowance will be paid, the frequency of payments and the period of payment;

(e) the arrangements and procedure for review, variation and termination of the allowance;

(f) the responsibilities of the agency under Regulation 6 with regard to arrangements for review, variation and termination of the allowance; and

(g) the responsibilities of the adopters with regard to their agreement under paragraph (4) of Regulation 2 to notify the agency of changes in their circumstances or those of the child.

## REVIEW, VARIATION AND TERMINATION OF ALLOWANCES

2.72. Once payment has commenced Regulation 6 requires the agency to review the allowance as follows:

(a) annually, after receiving a statement from the adopters giving information about their financial circumstances, the child's needs and resources, their address, and whether the child still has his home with them;

(b) at any other time, when the agency is notified by the adopters or otherwise of any change in the adopters' or child's circumstances.

2.73. Agencies should demonstrate flexibiity in responding to changes of circumstance and at the annual review. An allowance may increase or decrease as appropriate in an individual case. For example, a change of address involving higher housing costs may arise from a move to a home which is more appropriate to the needs of the adopted child. In other cases it may have no connection with the child's needs. Or, a deterioration in the child's condition may necessitate additional financial assistance. Conversely, a change in circumstance may result in a lower allowance or may result in the allowance being suspended until further review. In such a case, payment may recommence if circumstances again require the need for an allowance.

2.74. The adopters are required to complete and submit to the agency an annual statement of their circumstances. If they fail to do so, the agency may deem that the adopters need for an allowance has ceased until such time as the statement is supplied. Agencies should ensure that adopters are made aware of this provision by including it in the formal notification to adopters about adoption allowances.

2.75. For the purposes of the Regulations, relations between the adopters and the adoption agency exists essentially in respect of the allowance. Before the adoption order is made, the agency has a duty to supervise the placement of the child and submit a report to the court for the purpose of the adoption hearing. After the court order has been made, the status of the child in law in relation to the parents is exactly the same as that of any child born to that family. Provision of any post-adoption social work is independent from the administration of adoption allowances; neither is conditional upon the other.

2.76. There is no requirement or expectation that the agency should visit the adopters once the court order has been made. Notification of changes of circumstances and the annual review of the allowance do not normally necessitate direct contact between the agency and the adopters.

2.77. However, visits to the adoptive home, by agreement between the adopters and the agency, may be beneficial in certain circumstances. Some adopters may welcome an opportunity for contact with the agency. Agencies may wish to give adopters the option of a home visit, for example, before completion of the annual statement, so that the adopter and agency have an opportunity to discuss and evaluate the previous year's experiences. Arrangements for contact arising from agreed post-adoption services should not be confused with contact arising from payment of an allowance.

2.78. Regulation 6(5) provides for circumstances in which the agency shall terminate the allowance. These circumstances, which are similar to those in many adoption allowance schemes, are as follows:

(a) where the child ceases to have a home with the adopters. This applies where the child's departure from the adoptive home is considered to be permanent. It does not apply to periods of temporary absence away from the adoptive home – for example, in connection with education, respite care or hospitalisation;

(b) where the child ceases full-time education and commences employment or qualifies for a placement on a Government training scheme;

(c) where the child qualifies for income support or unemployment benefit in his own right;

(d) where the child reaches the age of 18, unless he remains in full-time education. In such a case, the allowance may continue until the child reaches the age of 21 so long as he continues in full time education;

(e) where any predetermined period agreed between the agency and the adopters expires.

Some agencies are now engaged in finding families for children whose parents are in the terminal stages of AIDS related illnesses. At first, these arrangements may be very 'open' adoption placements, with much contact between the child, the adoptive family and the dying birth parent. In circumstances such as these, an allowance could be paid for such a period, ending after the death of the birth parent, during which the need for an allowance is necessary as a result of arrangements for contact with the birth parent or emotional difficulties of the child.

It is recommended that, depending on the circumstances of the particular case, the agreed period be clearly and precisely framed at the beginning, even though it will not be possible to predict in advance the specific date when the period will end, and for the period to be reviewed at agreed intervals.

2.79. **The Regulations do not provide for an adoption allowance to recommence once it has been terminated.** Where there is doubt, therefore, whether a child has ceased to have a home with the adopters it is suggested that payments should be suspended rather than terminated.

# CONFIDENTIALITY, PRESERVATION AND ACCESS TO RECORDS

2.80. Regulation 7 provides that a record of each adoption allowance should be included with the adoption case records set up under Regulation 14(2) of the Adoption Agencies Regulations 1983. The record about the allowance should include details of any recommendation or decision made, including cases where the agency decides that no allowance is payable, either at the initial determination or resulting from an annual statement or change of circumstances. The record must be included with the case record relating to the child and the prospective adopter under Regulations 7(2)(a) and 9(3) of the Adoption Agencies Regulations and with any case records set up by the agency together.

2.81. As with other information on the adoption case records, the record about the allowance should be stored in a place of special security for at least

75 years. The record may be preserved on microfilm, provided the total record can be reproduced.

2.82. The record relating to the allowance is and must be treated as confidential. The only exceptions to the confidentiality requirement are those set out in Regulation 15 of the Adoption Agencies Regulations 1983. Where the agency receives a request for access or disclosure of information about the record relating to the allowance within the circumstances set out in Regulation 15 of those Regulations, the agency is required to comply with that request. However, as with existing requests for access to adoption case records under Regulation 15, the agency should satisfy itself about the genuineness of the request.

More detailed guidance on safekeeping, access and retention of records is contained in paragraphs 2.84–2.90 of Volume 3: 'Family Placements'.

# CHAPTER 3 THE ADOPTION CONTACT REGISTER AND INFORMATION ABOUT BIRTH RECORDS

## The Adoption Contact Register

### Purpose and function

3.1. The Registrar General is required to set up an Adoption Contact Register to enable adopted people to contact their birth parents and other relatives [section 51A of the Adoption Act 1976 as amended by Schedule 10 to the Children Act 1989]. Since 1975 adopted people over the age of eighteen years have been able to apply for access to their original birth record. This continues to be the case.

3.2. The information on a birth certificate includes the name of the birth mother and her address at that time; it may have her maiden name, if any, and possibly the name, address and occupation of the birth father. Using this information, some adopted people have been able to trace and make contact with their birth parents or other relatives. Until now, however, there have been few ways of learning whether contact would be welcome.

3.3. The purpose of the Adoption Contact Register is to put adopted people and their birth parents or other relatives in touch with each other where this is what they both want. The Register provides a safe and confidential way for birth parents and other relatives to assure an adopted person that contact would be welcome and give a current address.

3.4. The Register is operated on behalf of the Registrar General by the Office of Population Censuses and Surveys.

3.5. The Register is in two parts. Subject to the conditions in section 51A(4) of the Adoption Act 1976, the Registrar General will enter in Part 1 the name, current address and the details relating to the birth of an adopted person who wishes to contact his birth parent or other natural relatives. Subject to the conditions in section 51A(6) of the Act, the Registrar General will enter in Part 2 the name, current address and identifying details of a relative who wishes to contact an adopted person.

3.6. The Registrar General will send to the registered adopted person the name of any relative who has also registered together with the address which the relative has supplied. No information about the adopted person will be given to the relative except that the Registrar General will inform the relative when his details have been passed on to the adopted person.

### Role of local authorities

3.7. Local authorities are required to provide adoption counselling services under the arrangements of section 1 of the Adoption Act 1976. Authorities and approved adoption societies may also provide counselling services as specified in section 51 of the Act.

3.8. A booklet 'The Adoption Contact Register – Information for Adopted People and their Relatives' (ACR 110) is reproduced at Annex B and contains details about the operation of the Register and gives advice to adopted people and their relatives on how to use it.

## Change in approach

3.9. In the past it was thought best for all concerned that an adopted child's break with his birth family should be total. Parents who placed a child for adoption were generally told that a child would not have access to his birth records. The Adoption Act reflected increased understanding of the wishes and needs of adopted people. It recognised that although adoption makes a child a full member of a new family, information about his origins may still be important to an adopted person. The Children Act now extends these arrangements.

## Counselling

3.10. The local authority's counselling service has an important part to play in helping adopted people obtain information from their birth record. The booklet 'Access to Birth Records – Notes for Counsellors' (ACR 113) is intended to give counsellors in the United Kingdom as well as those operating abroad, advice about counselling adults who were adopted in the United Kingdom and who wish to have access to their birth records. It also contains information about the procedure to be followed to enable adopted people to obtain the information. This booklet is reproduced at Annex B.

3.11. People adopted before 12 November 1975 are required to see a counsellor before they can be given information from their original birth record. This is because in the years before 1975, some parents and adopters may have been led to believe that the children being adopted would never be able to find out their original names or the names of their parents. These arrangements were made in good faith and it is important that adopted people who want to find out more about their origins should understand what it may mean for them and for others.

3.12. People adopted after 11 November 1975 may choose whether or not to see a counsellor before being given the information.

3.13. The purpose of counselling is to give adopted people basic information about their adoption in a helpful manner, and to assist them to understand some of the possible effects on themselves and others of any further enquiries they may wish to make about their birth families.

3.14. The booklet 'Access to Birth Records – Information for Adopted People in the UK' (ACR 100) explains the provisions in adoption law, mainly the Adoption Act 1976, under which adopted people over the age of eighteen years can apply to the Registrar General for access to the original record of their birth. This booklet is reproduced at Annex B to this volume.

## People adopted in the UK and now living abroad

3.15. Up to now, people who were adopted in the United Kingdom and who subsequently settled abroad have been unable to exercise their right of access to their birth record because the Adoption Act made no provision for people to receive counselling except within the United Kingdom. This position is amended by the Children Act which enables people who were adopted before 12 November 1975 to take advantage of the access provisions without having to travel to the United Kingdom for a counselling interview.

3.16. For people who were adopted in the United Kingdom and who now live abroad, the booklet 'Access to Birth Records – Information for Adopted People Living Outside the United Kingdom' (ACR 101) explains the provisions of the Adoption Act, gives advice about counselling and how to go about obtaining information from their birth record. This booklet is reproduced at Annex B to this volume.

3.17. A companion booklet to ACR 101, 'Access to Birth Records – Counselling Organisations outside the United Kingdom' (ACR 114) – gives details of counselling organisations in Australia, Canada, New Zealand and South Africa. The information focuses on these countries since most of those who were adopted in the UK and are now living abroad reside in one of these four countries. This booklet is reproduced at Annex B to this volume.

3.18. Further copies of any of the five booklets referred to in this chapter are obtainable from:

Adoption Section
The General Registrar Office
Office of Population Censuses and Surveys
Smedley Hydro
Trafalgar Road
Birkdale
Southport PR8 2HH.

---

# STATUTORY INSTRUMENTS

---

**1991 No. 2030**

**CHILDREN AND YOUNG PERSONS**

**THE ADOPTION ALLOWANCE REGULATIONS 1991**

| | |
|---|---|
| *Made* | *9th September 1991* |
| *Laid before Parliament* | *12th September 1991* |
| *Coming into force* | *14th October 1991* |

The Secretary of State for Health, in exercise of the powers conferred by sections 9(2) and (3) and 57A of the Adoption Act 1976**(a)** and of all other powers enabling him in that behalf hereby makes the following Regulations:-

**Citation, commencement and interpretation**

**1.**–(1) These Regulations may be cited as the Adoption Allowance Regulations 1991 and shall come into force on 14th October 1991.

(2) In these Regulations unless the context otherwise requires –

"the Act" means the Adoption Act 1976;

"adopters" means the persons who have adopted or intend to adopt a child or, where there is only one such person, that person;

"adoption agency" means an approved adoption society or a local authority;

"adoption panel" means a panel established in accordance with regulation 5 of the Adoption Agencies Regulations 1983**(b)**;

"attendance allowance" means an allowance under section 35 of the Social Security Act 1975**(c)**;

"child benefit" means a benefit under section 1 of the Child Benefit Act 1975**(d)**;

"fostering allowance" means the amount of money paid by way of maintenance for a child placed with a foster parent pursuant to section 23(2)(a) or section 59(1)(a) of the Children Act 1989 (placement with foster parents and others by local authorities and voluntary organisations);

"income support" means income support under section 20 of the Social Security Act 1986**(e)**;

"mobility allowance" means an allowance under section 37A of the Social Security Act 1975;

"unemployment benefit" means unemployment benefit under section 14 of the Social Security Act 1975.

---

**(a)** 1976 c.36; section 57A was inserted by paragraph 25 of Schedule 10 to the Children Act 1989 (c.41).
**(b)** S.I. 1983/1964.
**(c)** 1975 c.14.
**(d)** 1975 c.61.
**(e)** 1986 c.50.

**[NOTE: Please refer to S.I. 1991 No.2130 in this Annex which amends part of these Regulations]**

(3) In these Regulations unless the context otherwise requires, a reference to a numbered regulation is to the regulation in these Regulations bearing that number, and a reference to a numbered paragraph is to the paragraph of that regulation bearing that number.

**Circumstances in which an allowance may be paid**

**2.**–(1) Without prejudice to paragraph (3), an allowance may be paid where one or more of the circumstances specified in paragraph (2) exists and the adoption agency –

(a) is making the arrangements for the child's adoption; and

(b) has decided –

    (i) in accordance with regulation 11(1) of the Adoption Agencies Regulations 1983 that the adoption by the adopters would be in the child's best interests, and

    (ii) after considering the recommendation of the adoption panel, that such adoption is not practicable without payment of an allowance.

(2) The circumstances referred to in paragraph (1) are –

(a) where the adoption agency is satisfied that the child has established a strong and important relationship with the adopters before the adoption order is made;

(b) where it is desirable that the child be placed with the same adopters as his brothers or sisters, or with a child with whom he has previously shared a home;

(c) where at the time of the placement for adoption the child –

    (i) is mentally or physically disabled or suffering from the effects of emotional or behavioural difficulties, and

    (ii) needs special care which requires a greater expenditure of resources that would be required if the child were not so disabled, or suffering from the effects of emotional or behavioural difficulties;

(d) where at the time of the placement for the adoption the child was mentally or physicaly disabled, or suffering from the effects of emotional or behavioural difficulties, and as a result at a later date he requires more care and a greater expenditure of resources than were required at the time he was placed for adoption because there is –

    (i) a deterioration in the child's health or condition, or

    (ii) an increase in his age; or

(e) where at the time of the placement for adoption it was known that there was a high risk that the child would develop an illness or disability and as a result at a later date he requires more care and a greater expenditure of resources than were required at the time he was placed for adoption because such illness or disability occurs.

(3) An allowance may be paid by the agency where before these Regulations come into force –

(a) an allowance was being paid by the agency to the adopters in respect of a child in accordance with a scheme which is revoked by section 57A(4) of the Act (revocation of schemes approved under section 57(4) of the Act) or under section 57(5)(b) of the Act (revocation of scheme by the Secretary of State) and the adopters have agreed to receive (instead of such allowance) an allowance complying with these Regulations, or

(b) the agency decided that the adopters are eligible to receive an allowance in accordance with a scheme which is revoked by section 57A(4) of the Act or under section 57(5)(b) of the Act and –

    (i) no payment has been made pursuant to that decision, and

    (ii) any conditions to which the agency's decision to pay such an allowance is subject are satisfied.

(4) In each case before an allowance is payable the adoption agency shall require the adopters to have agreed to –

    (a) inform the adoption agency immediately if –

        (i) the child no longer has his home with them (or either of them), if they have changed their address, or if the child dies, or

        (ii) there is any change in their financial circumstances or the financial needs or resources of the child; and

    (b) complete and supply the adoption agency with an annual statement of their financial circumstances and the financial circumstances of the child.

(5) An allowance may not be paid from a date before the date of placement for adoption and may be paid from such later date as may be determined by the adoption agency and notified to the adopters.

## Amount of the allowance

**3.**–(1) The allowance shall be of such amount as the adoption agency determines in accordance with paragraphs (2) to (4).

(2) In determining the amount of allowance the adoption agency shall take into account –

    (a) the financial resources available to the adopters including any financial benefit which would be available in respect of the child when adopted;

    (b) the amount required by the adopters in respect of their reasonable outgoings and commitments (excluding outgoings in respect of the child); and

    (c) the financial needs and resources of the child.

(3) In assessing the income available to the adopters the adoption agency shall disregard mobility and attendance allowance payable in respect of the child and, where the adopters are in receipt of income support, child benefit.

(4) The allowance paid by the adoption agency shall not –

    (a) include any element of remuneration for the care of the child by the adopters;

    (b) exceed the amount of the fostering allowance excluding any element of remuneration in that allowance which would be payable if the child was fostered by the adopters.

## Procedure in determining whether an allowance should be paid

**4.**–(1) Subject to paragraphs (2) and (3), an adoption agency shall, before an adoption order is made in respect of a child whose adoption they are arranging or have arranged –

    (a) consider whether an allowance may be paid in accordance with paragraphs (1) and (2) of regulation 2 (circumstances in which an allowance may be paid);

    (b) supply information to the adopters about allowances including the basis upon which amounts of allowances are determined;

    (c) give notice in writing in accordance with paragraph (4) to the adopters of their proposed decision as to whether an allowance should be paid and the proposed amount, if any, which would be payable;

    (d) consider any representations received from the adopters within the period specified in the notice;

    (e) make a decision as to whether an allowance should be paid, determine the amount, if any, which would be payable and notify the adopters of that decision and determination.

(2) The adoption agency shall not be required –

(a) in a case where the adopters may agree in accordance with regulation 2(3)(a) to receive payments complying with these Regulations instead of payments which are made to them in accordance with a scheme revoked by section 57A(4) of the Act (revocation of schemes approved under section 57(4) of the Act) or under section 57(5)(b) of the Act (revocation of scheme by the Secretary of State) –

(i) to comply with sub-paragraph (a) of paragraph (i),

(ii) to comply with sub-paragraph (b) of that paragraph before the adoption order is made provided that they do so as soon as is reasonably practicable after 14 October 1991, or

(iii) to comply with sub-paragraphs (c) to (e) of that paragraph unless and until an application is received by the adopters for an allowance to be made under these Regulations instead of under a scheme which has been revoked; or

(b) in a case where regulation 2(3)(b) applies, to comply with either of the following –

(i) sub-paragraph (a) of paragraph (1), or

(ii) sub-paragraphs (b) to (e) of that paragraph before an adoption order is made provided that they do so as soon as is reasonably practicable after 14 October 1991;

(c) in a case to which regulation 2(2)(d) or (e) of these Regulations applies, to determine the amount of an allowance unless or until –

(i) there is a deterioration in the child's health or condition, or an increase in his age, (in a case to which regulation 2(2)(d) applies) or

(ii) the onset of the illness or disability (in a case to which regulation 2(2)(e) applies,

and as a result the child requires more care and a greater expenditure of resources than were required at the time at which he was placed for adoption.

(3) An approved adoption society which holds itself out as not being an adoption agency which normally pays allowances shall not be required to comply with sub-paragraphs (a) and (b) of paragraph (1) and need comply with sub-paragraphs (c), (d) and (e) of that paragraph as respects any adopters only if they have considered whether or not to pay an allowance to those adopters.

(4) A notice under paragraph (1)(c) shall state the period of time within which the adopters may make representations to the adoption agency concerning the proposed decision or determination and the adoption agency shall not make a decision or determination under paragraph (1)(e) until after the expiry of that period.

## Information about allowances

**5.** After a decision has been made to pay an allowance, the adoption agency shall notify the adopters in writing of the following –

(a) the method of the determination of the amount of the allowance;

(b) the amount of the allowance as initially determined;

(c) the date of the first payment of the allowance;

(d) the method of payment of the allowance and frequency with which and the period for which payment will be made;

(e) the arrangements and procedure for review, variation and termination of the allowance;

(f) the responsibilities of –

(i) the agency under regulation 6, and

    (ii) the adopters pursuant to their agreement under paragraph (4) of regulation 2,

in respect of the allowance in the event of a change in circumstances of the adopters or the child.

## Review, variation and termination of allowances

**6.**–(1) The adoption agency shall review an allowance –

(a) annually, on receipt of a statement from the adopters as to –

    (i)   their financial circumstances;

    (ii)  the financial needs and resources of the child;

    (iii) their address and whether the child still has a home with them (or either of them); and

(b) if any change in the circumstances of the adopters or the child, including any change of address, comes to their notice.

(2) The adoption agency may vary or suspend payment of the allowance if, as a result of a review, they consider that, the adopters' need for it has changed or ceased since the amount of the allowance was last determined.

(3) Where the adopters fail to supply the adoption agency with an annual statement in accordance with their agreement under regulation 2(4)(b), the adoption agency may deem the adopters' need for an allowance to have ceased until such time as a statement is supplied.

(4) Where payment of an allowance is suspended the agency may recommence payment if as a result of a review the adoption agency considers that the financial circumstances of the adopters have become such that an allowance should be paid.

(5) The adoption agency shall terminate payment of an allowance when –

(a) the child ceases to have a home with the adopters (or either of them);

(b) the child ceases full-time education and commences employment or qualifies for a placement on a Government traning scheme;

(c) the child qualifies for income support or unemployment benefit in his own right;

(d) the child attains the age of eighteen, unless he continues in full-time education, when it may continue until he attains the age of twenty-one so long as he continues in full-time education; or

(e) any period agreed between the adoption agency and the adopters for the payment of the allowance expires.

## Confidentiality, preservation and access to records

**7.**–(1) Subject to regulation 15 of the Adoption Agencies Regulations 1983, any information obtained or recommendations received or decisions made by virtue of these Regulations shall be treated by the adoption agency as confidential.

(2) The adoption agency shall place a record of the details of each allowance in respect of a child including details of any determination under regulation 3 and review under regulation 6 on the case records that they are required to set up under the Adoption Agencies Regulations 1983.

Signed by authority of the Secretary of State for Health.

*Virginia Bottomley*
Minister of State,
Department of Health

9th September 1991

# EXPLANATORY NOTE

*(This note is not part of the Regulations)*

These Regulations make provision to enable adoption agencies to pay allowances to persons who have adopted or intend to adopt a child in pursuance of arrangements made by such agencies. They replace schemes approved by the Secretary of State under section 57(4) of the Adoption Act 1976 which are revoked in the coming into force of paragraph 25 of Schedule 10 to the Children Act 1989.

The Regulations make provision for persons who have already adopted a child and are in receipt of payments under a revoked scheme to receive instead, subject to their agreement, payments under these Regulations and for persons who have been found to be eligible for an allowance but who have not received payments under such schemes before these Regulations come into force (regulations 2(3) and 4(2)), for the other circumstances in which adoption agencies may pay allowances (regulation 2(1) and (2)) and in each case, the agreement of the adopters to supply the adoption agency with information which is required before an allowance may be paid, for determination of the amount of the allowance (regulation 3); for the procedure to be followed by adoption agencies before an adoption order is made in cases other than those where an allowance is being paid under a revoked scheme (regulation 4). This will require adoption agencies, amongst other things, to supply information to adopters about allowances (except where an approved adoption society holds itself out as not being an agency which normally pays allowances) and to consider representation from adopters.

They also make provision for certain information to be supplied to adopters by adoption agencies, for their responsibilities regarding review, variation and termination of allowances, after a decision to pay an allowance has been made (regulations 5 and 6) and for information and records of allowances to be placed on the case records kept by adoption agencies under the Adoption Agencies Regulations 1983 and to be treated as confidential in accordance with those Regulations (regulation 7).

*This Statutory Instrument is made to correct errors in S.I. 1991/2030 and is being issued free of charge to all known recipients of that Statutory Instrument.*

# STATUTORY INSTRUMENTS

### 1991 No. 2130

### CHILDREN AND YOUNG PERSONS

### THE ADOPTION ALLOWANCE
### (AMENDMENT) REGULATIONS 1991

| | |
|---|---|
| *Made* | *23rd September 1991* |
| *Laid before Parliament* | *23rd September 1991* |
| *Coming into force* | *14th October 1991* |

The Secretary of State for Health, in exercise of the powers conferred by section 57A of the Adoption Act 1976**(a)** and of all other powers enabling him in that behalf hereby makes the following Regulations:-

**Citation, commencement and interpretation**

 **1.**–(1)  These Regulations may be cited as the Adoption Allowance (Amendment) Regulations 1991 and shall come into force on 14th October 1991 immediately after the principal Regulations.

 (2)  In these Regulations "the principal Regulations" means the Adoption Allowance Regulations 1991**(b)**.

**Amendment of regulation 4(2) of the principal regulations**

 **2.**  Regulation 4(2) of the principal Regulations (exceptions from procedure in determining whether an allowance should be paid) shall be amended as follows –

- (a) in sub-paragraph (a)(i) of that regulation for "paragraph (i)" there shall be substituted "paragraph (1)";
- (b) in sub-paragraph (a)(iii) of that regulation for "adopters" there shall be substituted "agency".

Signed by authority of the Secretary of State for Health.

*Stephen Dorrell*
Parliamentary Under-Secretary of State,
Department of Health

23rd September 1991

---

**(a)** 1976 c.36; section 57A was inserted by paragraph 25 of Schedule 10 to the Children Act 1989 (c.41).
**(b)** S.I. 1991/2030.

## EXPLANATORY NOTE

*(This note is not part of the Regulations)*

These Regulations amend regulation 4(2) of the Adoption Allowance Regulations 1991 (exceptions from procedure to be followed in determining whether an allowance should be paid) by correcting the reference to "paragraph (i)" in sub-paragraph (a)(i) to "paragraph (1)" and the reference to "adopters" in sub-paragraph (a)(iii) to "agency".

## SCHEDULE 10

Section 88.

AMENDMENTS OF ADOPTION LEGISLATION

### PART 1

AMENDMENTS OF ADOPTION ACT 1976 (C. 36)

**25.** After section 57 there shall be inserted –

"Permitted allowances.

**57A.**–(1) The Secretary of State may make regulations for the purpose of enabling adoption agencies to pay allowances to persons who have adopted, or intend to adopt, children in pursuance of arrangements made by the agencies.

(2) Section 57(1) shall not apply to any payment made by an adoption agency in accordance with the regulations.

(3) The regulations may, in particular, make provision as to –

(a) the procedure to be followed by any agency in determining whether a person should be paid an allowance;

(b) the circumstances in which an allowance may be paid;

(c) the factors to be taken into account in determining the amount of an allowance;

(d) the procedure for review, variation and termination of allowances; and

(e) the information about allowances to be supplied by any agency to any person who is intending to adopt a child.

(4) Any scheme approved under section 57(4) shall be revoked as from the coming into force of this section.

SCH. 10

(5) Section 57(1) shall not apply in relation to any payment made –

(a) in accordance with a scheme revoked under subsection (4) or section 57(5)(b); and

(b) to a person to whom such payments were made before the revocation of the scheme.

(6) Subsection (5) shall not apply where any person to whom any payments may lawfully be made by virtue of subsection (5) agrees to receive (instead of such payments) payments complying with regulations made under this section."

# THE ADOPTION CONTACT REGISTER

## INFORMATION FOR ADOPTED PEOPLE AND THEIR RELATIVES

A NEW FRAMEWORK FOR THE CARE
AND UPBRINGING OF CHILDREN

ACR 110

1.     The Children Act 1989 provides for the Registrar General to operate an Adoption Contact Register.  This leaflet explains the background to the introduction of the Register on 1 May 1991 and describes the way it works.  There are notes on:

- how to use the Register if **you were adopted** and how to use it if you are a **birth parent or other relative** of an adopted person;

- the possibility of using the address of a third party (an intermediary) through which contact can be made;

- what happens when there is a link on the Register between an adopted person and a relative.

    A list of organisations and agencies offering advice, counselling and intermediary services appears at the end of the leaflet.

    For the purposes of the Register, 'relative' includes the adopted person's birth parents and anyone related to that person by blood, half blood or marriage: it does not include those who are relatives as a result of adoption.

2.    Since 1975 adopted adults have been able to apply for access to their original birth record. This does not change. The information on a birth certificate includes the name of the birth mother and her address at that time: it may have her maiden name, if any, and possibly the name, address and occupation of the birth father. Using this information, some adopted people have been able to trace and make contact with their birth parents or other relatives. But until now there have been few ways of learning whether contct would be welcome. A register provides a safe and confidential way for birth parents and other relatives to assure an adopted person that contact would be welcome and to give a current address.

3.    The Register is in two parts. Part I is a list of adopted people and Part II is a list of birth parents and other relatives of an adopted person. The Registrar General will send to an adopted person on the Register the name of any relatives who have also registered, together with the address supplied by the relative, and tell the relative that this has been done. No information about the adopted person can be given to a birth parent or other relative. A registration fee is payable for entry in the Adoption Contact Register.

4. The purpose of the Adoption Contact Register is to put adopted people and their birth parents or other relatives in touch with each other **where this is what they both want.** Birth parents and other relatives who have decided that they would prefer not to have contact with an adopted person need have no fear that the introduction of the Register will put them at greater risk of an unwanted approach. The Register cannot help an adopted person to learn of the whereabouts of a birth parent or other relative unless that person has chosen to be entered on the Register. The Registrar General can only pass on a name and address if and when that name and address are supplied to him.

5. The introduction of the Register cannot, of course, prevent an adopted person from trying to find a birth parent, just as an adopted person can do at present, even though the birth parent has not applied for entry on the Register. If you are worried than an approach from a son or daughter or other relative who was adopted could cause you difficulties it may be helpful and reassuring to discuss your anxieties with an experienced counsellor.

6. 'Contact' may have different meanings for different people using the Register. Contact may be assumed by one person to be an open invitation to visit. Another person may see contact as an exchange of information, possibly through a third party and not including any meetings. Between these two extremes there can be many variations. You should be prepared for the possibility that the expectations of the adopted person and the relative may differ.

7. The Registrar General cannot pass letters or any information between adopted people and their relatives, beyond a name and address. However, some relatives may prefer initial contact to be limited to exchanges of letters or information. If this applies to you, you may ask the Registrar General to register you under the address of an organisation which will act as an intermediary between you and the adopted person. There is further information and advice about this in paragraphs 17 - 20.

3

**ADOPTED PEOPLE**

8.  An adopted person must be at least eighteen years old to use the Register. The Registrar General must hold the record of his or her birth. It is not essential for the adoption order to have been made in England or Wales. The Registrar General would be prepared to advise in individual cases. If, however, either the birth or the adoption took place in Scotland a separate voluntary service is provided and information can be obtained from Birth Link, Family Care, 21 Castle Street, Edinburgh EH2 3DN.

9.  To be able to complete the application form you will need to have some information about your birth including:

    • the name in which your birth was registered before you were adopted
    • your date and place (town, village or district) of birth
    • your birth mother's name and surname
    • your birth mother's maiden name and birth father's name if these were included in your original birth entry

10. If you do not have this information your adoptive parents may be able to tell you. Otherwise you can apply for access to your birth record. The leaflet 'Access to Birth Records: Information for Adopted People in the UK' (ACR 100) explains the procedure and can be obtained from the Registrar General at the address given in paragraph 16. A separate leaflet will be available by October 1991 for people living outside the UK who would like to have access to their birth records in their own country. Any adopted adult can be given birth records information. This does not depend upon a relative being included on the Adoption Contact Register and no fee is charged.

11. When you are entered on the Register, it may be discovered that a relative has already registered. If this happens you will be sent the name and address supplied by the relative and a note of his or her relationship to you. If no relative has registered you will only receive an acknowledgement of your registration. However, you will be sent details of any relative who subsequently registers. This may happen quite soon or it could be many years later, or may not happen at all. It is therefore most important that you keep the Registrar General informed of any change of name or address.

## BIRTH PARENTS AND OTHER RELATIVES

12. A relative who wishes to be included in Part II (relatives) of the register must provide evidence of his or her relationship to the adopted person. A birth mother may easily prove her relationship by providing a copy of her birth certificate*, her child's birth certificate, and if she was married after the birth of her child, a copy of her marriage certificate. Other relatives may have to provide additional certificates in order to prove their relationship.

13. A birth father who was not married to the baby's mother may not have been included in the original birth record and may have difficulty in proving his relationship to the adopted person. An affiliation or other court order declaring paternity would be acceptable evidence but the absence of such orders need not necessarily prevent entry in Part II of the Register. The Registrar General will be please to advise in individual cases. In some cases it may be necessary to seek legal advice.

14. To be able to complete an application form and so that the Registrar General may identify your relative who was adopted, you must provide full details of his or her birth. You will need to know:

   • the name in which his or her birth was registered before being adopted

   • the date and place (town, village or district) of birth

   • the birth mother's name

   • the birth mother's maiden name and birth father's name if these were included in the original birth entry.

---

*her full adoption certificate if she was herself adopted

5

The Registrar General will acknowledge your registration when he has established your relationship to the adopted person and has been able to locate the birth record from the information you supplied.

15.  Just as an adopted person cannot receive information from the Register unless a relative has provided information, so the information which a relative has provided cannot be sent to the adopted person unless he or she chooses to register. This could happen quite soon or it could happen after many years or it may not happen at all. Although this may be very disappointing there is no other action which the Registrar General can take. You may find it helpful to discuss all the implications with a counsellor.

16.  **Application forms for adopted people and for relatives** can be obtained by writing to the Registrar General at:

>  **Office of Population Censuses and Surveys**
>  The General Register Office
>  Adoptions Section
>  Smedley Hydro
>  Trafalgar Road, Birkdale
>  Southport  PR8 2HH

The registration fee should be sent with the completed application form. The Registrar General will return all birth and marriage certificates and other original personal documents to you after inspection. If he needs any more certificates to prove your claim he will ask for them.

If you change your mind about registration, you should write to the Registrar General asking him to remove your name and address from the Register. Twenty eight days notice is required. **Please remember: while your name remains on the Register, it is important to let the Registrar General know if you change your address.**

# USING AN ADDRESS OTHER THAN YOUR OWN

17. The Adoption Contact Register has been set up to help adopted people and their birth parents and other relatives make contact. It may seem strange that therefore some relatives of adopted people may want to register an address other than their own. However, some people may have good reasons for doing so. That is why the Registrar General is able to register an address 'through which contact can be made' as an alternative to a relative's home address. An alternative address supplied should be that of an organisation or individual such as a social worker or counsellor who has agreed to act as an intermediary. The organisations listed at 22. have agreed in principle to provide this service. Any relative who would prefer to learn of a Register link through a third person, with support available if needed, can consider using the address of such an intermediary. If you are happy to register your own address, the adopted person can choose to approach you direct.

18.     An **adopted person** will receive the name and address supplied by the relative which may be either the relative's own address or that of an intermediary. The Registrar will advise the **relative** that the information has been sent to the adopted person. It will then be up to the adopted person to act on the information. However, deciding at this stage to take no action, even through a third party, may cause disappointment and is not the purpose of the Register.

19.     An adopted person who received a relative's home address should act sensitively and with care. It may be tempting to telephone a relative or just turn up at his or her home. This may not be a good idea as the adopted person will have no knowledge of the relative's circumstances. Discussion with a counsellor can help as he or she will be able to suggest helpful ways of proceeding.

20.     There may be disappointment at first if a relative has supplied an address which is not his or her own. It should not be assumed that this has been done to avoid anyone. He or she may feel a need for support in establishing contact. Using an intermediary is a way of ensuring that help is at hand. An intermediary will try to help obtain the information which is most important and his or her experience in acting as a 'go-between' in these circumstances can be very useful.

21.    All local authority Social Services Departments provide counselling for people who have any problems concerning adoption: this includes adopted people, birth parents and adoptive parents. You should contact your local Social Services Department for details of services available.

Voluntary adoption societies provide counselling in connection with adoptions they have arranged. If you are involved with an adoption arranged by an adoption society you can contact the society for discussion and advice. This applies whether you are an adopted person, a birth parent or an adoptive parent.

**Parent to Parent Information on Adoption Services (PPIAS)**
Lower Boddington
Daventry
Northants NN11 6YB

PPIAS is a support group for adoptive families. The National Co-ordinator is pleased to talk to anyone involved in adoption and will be especially willing to discuss the implications of the Adoption Contact Register for adoptive parents.

22. **ORGANISATIONS WHICH WILL PROVIDE INTERMEDIARY AND COUNSELLING SERVICES AND WHOSE ADDRESS MAY BE USED FOR REGISTRATIONS IF REQUESTED**

**Natural Parents Support Group (NPSG)**
Contact Register Section c/o Ms D Ward
10 Alandale Crescent
Garforth
Leeds LS25 1DH

**National Organisation for Counselling Adoptees and their Parents (NORCAP)**
3 New High Street
Headington
Oxford OX3 7AJ

**The Post Adoption Centre**
8 Torriano Mews
Torriano Avenue
Kentish Town
London NW5 2RZ

23. These organisations will be happy to provide an intermediary service for you but please contact them before completing the Adoption Contact Register Application to make sure you have their correct address and that they know how to reach you should there be some news to pass on. Some adoption agencies and regional post adoption centres may also agree to provide this service for their clients. **It is important to reach clear agreement in advance with any intermediary whose address is to be registered.** Please remember to notify your intermediary of any change of address. A fee or donation will generally be required as a contribution towards the cost of providing a service. You should discuss this with the organisation of your choice.

Prepared by Department of Health

JA45/1 6/91

# ACCESS TO BIRTH RECORDS

## INFORMATION FOR ADOPTED
## PEOPLE IN THE UK

THE CHILDREN ACT 1989

A NEW FRAMEWORK FOR THE CARE
AND UPBRINGING OF CHILDREN

ACR 100

# FOREWORD

This leaflet provides information to people adopted in the UK and who either continue to live in the UK or are living overseas but who intend to travel to the UK for counselling.

A separate leaflet will be available shortly for people living outside the UK who would like to have access to their birth records in their own country. New arrangements to be introduced on 14 October 1991 will enable people who were adopted before 12 November 1975 to receive the necessary counselling in the country in which they live.

This leaflet explains the provisions in adoption law, chiefly the Adoption Act 1976, under which adopted adults (at least 18 years of age) can apply to the Registrar General for access to the original record of their birth.

# BACKGROUND

In the past it was thought best for all concerned that an adopted child's break with his birth family should be total. Parents who placed a child for adoption were generally told that a child would not have access to his birth record. The current legislation reflects increased understanding of the wishes and needs of adopted people. It recognises that although adoption makes a child a full member of a new family, information about his or her origins may still be important to an adopted person.

People adopted before 12 November 1975 are required to see a counsellor before they can be given access to their records because in the years before 1975, some parents and adopters may have been led to believe that the children being adopted would never be able to find out their original names or the names of their parents. These arrangements were made in good faith and it is important that adopted people who want to find out more about their origins should understand what it may mean for them and for others.

This means that *if you were adopted before 12 November 1975,* you will have to see an experienced social worker called a counsellor before you can obtain information from your original birth record.

*If you were adopted after 11 November 1975,* you may choose whether or not you would like to see a counsellor before you are given the information which will lead you to your birth record.

# THE PURPOSE OF COUNSELLING

The purpose of counselling is:

- to give adopted people basic information about their adoption in a helpful manner, and

- to help adopted people to understand some of the possible effects on themselves and others of any further enquiries they may wish to make about their birth families.

# HOW AND WHERE TO APPLY

You should complete the application form for access to birth records. If you do not already have a form, you can obtain one by writing to the Registrar General at:

   The Office of Population Censuses and Surveys

   The General Register Office

   Adoptions Section

   Smedley Hydro

   Trafalgar Road, Birkdale

   Southport PR8 2HH

The form asks you for some details of your adoption so that your records can be traced.

You should send your completed application form to the above address. When the Registrar General receives your application form he will write to you about the next step. All applications are, of course, treated in strictest confidence.

# PLACES WHERE YOU CAN MEET A COUNSELLOR

You are asked to choose where you would prefer to meet a counsellor. You may choose between:

- The General Register Office;
  the appointment will be arranged at St. Catherine's House, 10 Kingsway, London WC2. This will be done as quickly as possible but it may take a few weeks;

- the local authority, regional or island council (Scotland), or Health and Social Services Board (Northern Ireland) in whose area you are living;

- any other local authority, council (Scotland) or Board (Northern Ireland); or

- if your adoption was arranged by an approved adoption society, by that society.

If you have any difficulty, please see the application form and/or ask the local Citizens' Advice Bureau who will advise you about the names and addresses of local authorities and adoption societies.

# MEETING THE COUNSELLOR

You will understand that it is very important that precautions are taken against information about you being given to an unauthorised person. To avoid this you must take with you some means of identification, such as a bank card, a passport/identity card or a driving licence.

3

# WHAT THE COUNSELLOR CAN TELL YOU

The Registrar General will have sent the counsellor most of the information from your adoption order.  This includes:

- your original name;

- the name of your birth mother;

- possibly, but not certainly, the name of your birth father;

- the name of the court where the order was made.

The counsellor will give you this information at your request.

The counsellor will not have a copy of your original birth record at the interview but will be able to give you the necessary application form.  You can use the information which the counsellor will give you and the application form to apply for a copy of your original birth record at any time if you decide you want one.  There is a standard charge for this birth certificate.

# BIRTH RECORDS

A certificate of birth provides the following information:

- the date and place of your birth;

- the name under which you were originally registered;

- your mother's name and perhaps her occupation;

- the name and address of the person who registered the birth;

- the date of registration;

- the name of the registrar.

It may or may not give your father's name and occupation.  If a child's parents are not married to each other, the father's name is not always on the birth certificate.

# FURTHER INFORMATION

Whether or not additional information exists which could be made available to you depends on a number of things, including how your adoption was arranged.

Your adoption could have been arranged through an adoption society or a local authority. Or, if you were adopted before most private adoption arrangements were prohibited, your adoption could have been arranged through an individual such as a doctor, a solicitor or a friend. Or your mother might have arranged it on her own, privately. Some children are adopted by grandparents or other relatives and there have also been a very large number of adoptions by a birth parent with a step-parent.

If your adoption was arranged through an adoption society or a local authority, they may have records. Also, local authorities may have information about adoptions which took place in their area even though they did not arrange them. The counsellor will not have this information but will be able to give you an authorisation to ask the court which made your adoption order for the name of the adoption society or local authority, if any, that took part in the arrangements for your adoption. If the court records are still available and the court is able to give you the name of the adoption society or local authority concerned, you will be able to follow up your enquiries with them. If you were adopted after 12 November 1975 and have decided not to have counselling, you can obtain an authorisation from the Registrar General whose address is given above.

To avoid disappointment, however, it must be said that there can be no certainty that any additional information about your adoption or background still exists. Before 1984, adoption agencies were only required to keep their records for twenty five years and the court records are not kept indefinitely. Local authorities' records may not go back far enough to include people whose adoption took place many years ago, or they may have been lost or destroyed.

Unfortunately too, old records are often brief so that information you may want to have may not be included. However much they want to help, the organisations involved may not, for one reason or another, be able to give you the information you would like.

Although you may not be able to get all the information you would like, these arrangements will make sure that you get some basic facts about your birth mother and perhaps your birth father too.

# IF YOU DECIDE NOT TO SEE A COUNSELLOR

If you were adopted after 11 November 1975 and indicate on your application form that you do not wish to see a counsellor, the information will be sent direct to you by the Registrar General. You will receive:

- the name of the court which made the adoption order and the number, if any, of the adoption application;

- the name of your birth mother and, if applicable, your birth father.

This information will enable you to apply for a copy of your original birth record at any time. There is a standard charge for this birth certificate.

You will also receive a copy of the authorisation form which will enable you, if you wish, to ask the court which made the adoption order for the name of the local authority or adoption society, if any, that took part in the arrangements for your adoption (see further information).

# ADOPTION CONTACT REGISTER

You may be interested to know that the Registrar General also maintains at the General Register Office an Adoption Contact Register, the purpose of which is to put adopted persons and their relatives in touch with each other if this is their stated wish. Further information about this Register is contained in leaflet 'The Adoption Contact Register' (ACR 110) available from the Registrar General at the above address.

Prepared by Department of Health and OPCS
Printed in UK April 1991.

# ACCESS

## TO

# BIRTH RECORDS

## INFORMATION FOR ADOPTED
## PEOPLE LIVING OUTSIDE THE
## UNITED KINGDOM

A NEW FRAMEWORK FOR THE CARE
AND UPBRINGING OF CHILDREN

ACR101

This leaflet provides information to people who were adopted in the United Kingdom (UK) but who are living outside the UK and would like to have access to their birth records in their own country.

It explains the provisions in adoption law, chiefly the Adoption Act 1976, under which adopted adults (at least 18 years of age) can apply to the Registrar General for access to the original record of their birth. The leaflet also explains new arrangements to be introduced on 14 October 1991 in England and Wales which will enable people who were adopted in the UK before 12 November 1975 to receive statutory counselling in the country in which they live. Statutory counselling is not required where the person was adopted in Scotland.

A separate leaflet, ACR 100, is available for people adopted in the UK who either continue to live in the UK or who are living overseas but intend to travel to the UK for counselling.

The information in this leaflet does not apply to persons whose birth records are kept by the Registrar General in Northern Ireland. Any such person who wish to be advised about their position with regard to obaining access to their birth record should write to :-

The Registrar General
Oxford House
49-55 Chichester Street
Belfast
Northern Ireland
BT1 4HL.

# THE LEGAL RIGHTS OF ADOPTED PEOPLE OVER EIGHTEEN YEARS OF AGE

In the years since 1975, adults of at least 18 years of age who were adopted in the UK have been able to apply to the Registrar General for access to the original record of their birth. People adopted in England or Wales before 12 November 1975 are required to see a counsellor before they can be given access to their records. Adopted people living outside UK have frequently been unable to exercise their right of access to their birth record because the Adoption Act 1976 made no provision for people to receive this counselling except within the UK. Certain provisions of the Children Act 1989, which come into effect on 14 October 1991 amend the Adoption Act to remedy this position. The new provisions enable people who were adopted in England or Wales before 12 November 1975 to take advantage of the access provisions without having to travel to the UK for a counselling interview.

# BACKGROUND

In the past it was thought best for all concerned that an adopted child's break with his birth family should be total. Parents who placed a child for adoption were generally told that the child would not have access to his birth record. The current legislation reflects increased understanding of the wishes and needs of adopted people. It recognises that although adoption makes a child a full member of a new family, information about his or her origins may still be important to the adopted person.

The reason the law in England and Wales requires people adopted before 12 November 1975 to see a counsellor before they can be given access to their records is that, in the past, some parents and adopters may have been led to believe that the children being adopted would never be able to find out their original names or the names of their parents. These arrangements were made in good faith and it is important that adopted people who want to find out more about their origins should understand what it may mean for them and for others.

Consequently, **if you were adopted in England or Wales before 12 November 1975** you will have to see an experienced social worker called a counsellor before you can be given information from your original birth record.

**If you were adopted in the UK after 11 November 1975**, there is no legal requirement for you to see a counsellor. However, if you are in the UK and wish to see a counsellor, a counselling service is available.

# THE PURPOSE OF COUNSELLING

The purpose of counselling is:
- to give adopted people basic information about their adoption, and
- to help adopted people understand some of the possible effects on themselves and others of any further enquiries they may wish to make about their birth families.

3

If you were adopted in England or Wales, you should complete the application form for access to birth records. If you do not already have a form, you can obtain one from:

The Office of Population Censuses and Surveys
The General Register Office
Adoptions Section
Smedley Hydro
Trafalgar Road
Birkdale
Southport
PR8 2HH
England

The form asks you for some details of your adoption so that your records can be traced. It also asks you to supply details about the body or organisation within your country of residence which has agreed to carry out your counselling interview.

You should send your completed application form to the above address. When the Registrar General receives your application form he will write to you about the next step. All applications are, or course, treated in strictest confidence.

If you were adopted in Scotland, you can obtain an application form from
The General Register Office (Scotland)
Adoption Section
New Register House
Edinburgh
EH1 3YT
Scotland

# PLACES WHERE YOU CAN MEET A COUNSELLOR

If you were adopted in England or Wales, counselling will be provided by a body or organisation which the Registrar General is satisfied is suitable to provide counselling. The organisation will need to notify the Registrar General that it is prepared to carry out the counselling interview.

The companion leaflet ACR 114 gives details of organisations approved by the Registrar General. If you live in a country which is not included in the supplement, you should contact a counselling organisation in your own country. There may be a fee for counselling. You should include with your application form to the Registrar General details of the organisation (ie history, experience of adoption counselling, whether officially approved) for the Registrar General's consideration. This information will normally be supplied to you by the organisation concerned.

If you are in the UK or visiting the UK, counselling can be arranged at one of the places listed in leaflet ACR 100. Adequate notice of your visit to this country should be given so that arrangements can be made in advance.

# MEETING THE COUNSELLORS

You will understand that it is very important that precautions need to be taken to ensure that information about you is not given to unauthorised persons. So, to avoid this, you must take with you some means of identification, such as a medical card, a passport/identity card or a driving licence.

## WHAT THE COUNSELLOR CAN TELL YOU

Provided the Registrar General is satisfied about the body or organisation which has agreed to provide counselling for you, the Registrar General will have sent the counsellor the following information from your birth record. This includes:

- your original name;
- the name of your birth mother;
- possibly, but not certainly, the name of your birth father;
- the name of the court where the order was made.

The counsellor will give you this information at your request.

The counsellor will not have a copy of your original birth certificate at the interview but will be able to give you the necessary application form. You can use the information which the counsellor will give you and the application form to apply for a copy of your original birth record at any time. There is a standard charge for this birth certificate.

## BIRTH RECORDS

A certificate of birth provides the following information:

- the date and place of your birth;
- the name under which you were originally registered;
- your mother's name and perhaps her occupation;
- your parent(s) address at that time;
- the name and address of the person who registered the birth (this is usually the mother);
- the date of registration;
- the name of the registrar.

It may or may not give your father's name and occupation. If a child's parents are not married to each other, the father's name is not always in the birth record.

6

# IF YOU WERE ADOPTED AFTER 11 NOVEMBER 1975

If you were adopted after 11 November 1975 and indicate on your application form that you do not wish to see a counsellor in the UK, you may apply direct to the Registrar General for information about your birth. The Registrar General will send direct to you:-

- the name of the court which made the adoption order and the number, if any, of the adoption application;

- the name of your birth mother and, if applicable, your birth father.

This information will enable you to apply for a copy of your original birth record at any time. There is a standard charge for this birth certificate.

You will also receive a copy of the authorisation form which will enable you, if you wish, to ask the court which made the adoption order for the name of the local authority or adoption society, if any, that took part in the arrangements for your adoption (see further information).

Whether or not additional information exists which could be made available to you depends on a number of things, including how your adoption was arranged.

Your adoption could have been arranged through an adoption society or a local authority. Or if you were adopted before most private adoption arrangements were prohibited, your adoption could have been arranged through an Individual such as a doctor, a solicitor, or a friend. Or your mother might have arranged it on her own, privately. Some children are adopted by grandparents or other relatives and there have also been a very large number of adoptions by a birth parent with a step-parent.

If your adoption was arranged through an adoption society or a local authority, they may have records. Local authorities may also have information about adoptions which took place in their area even though they did not arrange them. The counsellor will not have this information but will be able to give you an authorisation to ask the court which made your adoption order for the name of the adoption society or local authority, if any, that took part in the arrangements for your adoption. If the court records are still available and the court is able to give you the name of the adoption society or local authority concerned, you will be able to follow up your enquiries with them. If you were adopted in Scotland, or in England and Wales after 11 November 1975, and have decided not to have counselling you can obtain an authorisation from the Registrar General whose address is given above.

To avoid disappointment however, it must be said that there can be no certainty that any additional information about your adoption or background still exists. Before 1984, adoption agencies were only required to keep their records for twenty five years and court records are not kept indefinitely. Local authorities' records may not go back far enough to include people whose adoption took place many years ago, or they may have been lost or destroyed.

Unfortunately too, old records are often brief so that the information you may want may not be included. However much they want to help, the organisations involved may not, for one reason or another, be able to give you the information you would like.

Although you may not be able to get all the information you would like, these arrangements will make sure that you get some basic facts about your birth mother and perhaps your birth father too.

## ADOPTION CONTACT REGISTER

You may be interested to know that the Registrar General also maintains at the General Register Office an Adoption Contact Register, the purpose of which is to put adopted persons and their relatives in touch with each other if this is their stated wish. Further information about the Register, for both adopted persons and their relatives, is contained in leaflet ACR 110 available from the Registrar General at the above address. For people adopted in Scotland, a separate voluntary service is provided and information can be obtained from Birth Link, Family Care, 21 Castle Street, Edinburgh EH2 3DN, Scotland.

ACR 101

Prepared by Department of Health

Printed in the UK September 1991.

# ACCESS

## TO

# BIRTH RECORDS

## NOTES FOR COUNSELLORS

A NEW FRAMEWORK FOR THE CARE
AND UPBRINGING OF CHILDREN

ACR113

# FOREWORD

This leaflet gives information to counsellors who provide counselling to adults (those over 18 years of age) who were adopted in the United Kingdom and who wish to have access to their birth records. It is one of a series of leaflets issued in connection with the introduction, on 14 October 1991, of the Children Act 1989. Details of the other leaflets are included in the text.

It is intended for counsellors

(a) in the UK who are either required, or who may be asked, to provide counselling to adopted people at one of the places in the UK specified in adoption legislation; and

(b) outside the UK who are able to provide a counselling service to adopted people in the country in which they are living. The Registrar General for England and Wales must be satisfied that any counselling body or organisation outside the UK is suitable to provide adoption counselling.

Leaflet ACR 114 "Access to Birth Records: Counselling Organisations Outside the United Kingdom" gives details of organisations approved by the Registrar General.

This leaflet includes information about adoption legislation, the role of the counsellor and the procedure to enable adopted people to have access to their birth record. Details about adoption arrangements which may be of particular assistance to counsellors outside the UK are reproduced in the Appendices.

The information in this leaflet is not applicable to persons whose birth records are kept by the Registrar General in Northern Ireland. Any such person who wishes to be informed of their position with regard to obtaining access to their birth record should write to:-

The Registrar General
Oxford House
49-55 Chichester Street
Belfast
Northern Ireland
BT1 4HL

# LEGAL RIGHTS FOR PEOPLE ADOPTED IN THE UK

In the years since 1975, adults (at least 18 years of age in England and Wales, 17 in Scotland) who were adopted in the UK have been able to apply to the Registrar General for access to the original record of their birth. On adoption, an entry is made in the Adopted Children Register in the child's new name from which certificates are available; and the information which links his new name with his original birth record is kept confidential by the Registrar General (see Appendix A). It is this information which the law requires the Registrar General to give to adopted persons over 18 who apply for their birth particulars. For the reasons explained below, however, the law also provides that those adopted in England or Wales before 12 November 1975 have to attend an interview with a counsellor before they can be given the information.

Adopted people living outside the UK have frequently been unable to exercise the right of access to their birth record in England or Wales because adoption law made no provision for people to receive this counselling except within the UK. Certain provisions of the Children Act 1989, which come into effect on 14 October 1991, amend the law to remedy this position. The new provisions enable people who were adopted before 12 November 1975 to take advantage of the access provisions without having to travel to Great Britain for a counselling interview. The relevant sections in the legislation - the Adoption Act 1976 as amended by the Children Act 1989 - is set out in Appendix B. People adopted in Scotland, either before or after 12 November 1975, are not required to receive such counselling.

It has always been possible for adopted persons to obtain copies of their birth records if they already knew their original name - for example, if their adoptive parents had shared this information with them. Before 1975, persons adopted in England and Wales were able to get their birth record only if a court agreed to make an order requiring the Registrar General to supply a certified copy of their original birth record. In Scotland adopted people have always been able to get a copy of their original birth certificate at age 17.

In 1975, when Parliament was debating the proposals to give adopted adults access to their birth records, considerable concern was expressed about making the legislation retrospective since this would alter arrangements which had been made in good faith in the past. Many birth parents had given up children and adopters had adopted them on the understanding that the children would not have access to their birth records. Parliament therefore decided, that all persons over 18 who were adopted in England and Wales before the legislation was passed on 12 November 1975 and who wanted information from their birth records should be required to have a meeting with a counsellor before they could be given the information to enable them to obtain a birth certificate. For those adopted on or after 12 November 1975 counselling is optional.

# THE PURPOSE OF COUNSELLING

The object is

- to give adopted people basic information about adoption; and

- to help adopted people to understand some of the possible effects on themselves and others of any further enquiries they may wish to make about their birth families.

# PROCEDURE

The leaflet 'Access to Birth Records: Information For Adopted People in the UK' (ACR 100) explains the provisions and the counselling arrangements as they apply to adopted people who are either living in the UK or who intend to travel to the UK for counselling. The leaflet is available from the Registrar General at:

The General Register Office
Adoptions Section
Smedley Hydro
Trafalgar Road
Birkdale
Southport
PR8 2HH
England

Copies are also available, in the UK, from Social Services Departments, adoption societies, relevant voluntary organisations and Citizens Advice Bureaux.

The leaflet 'Access to Birth Records: Information for Adopted People Living Outside the UK' (ACR 101) available from the General Registrar Office explains the arrangements which apply to those who wish to receive counselling in their own country.

3

The application form, also available from the Registrar General, asks the applicant for details of his adoption which he will be able to supply from his adoption certificate. It also asks him to indicate where he would like to receive counselling. On receiving the application form, the General Register Office will trace the adopted person's records in the indices to the Adopted Children Register and will extract the birth particulars and send them to the counsellor. If the applicant has chosen to see a counsellor at the General Register Office in London, he will be informed of the arrangements that have been made for an interview. If he has chosen to see a counsellor elsewhere in the UK, he will be informed that the information he seeks has been sent to the Director of Social Services of the local authority concerned, the Regional or Island Council (in Scotland) or the Health and Social Services Board (in Northern Ireland); or the approved adoption society which arranged the adoption.

Separate specimen application forms for access to birth records for a person adopted before 12 November 1975 or a person adopted after 11 November 1975 are reproduced at Appendix C.

If the applicant wishes to see a counsellor in his own country, the Registrar General will need to be satisfied that the body or organisation which the applicant has contacted is suitable and willing to provide counselling to the applicant.

The companion leaflet, ACR 114, gives details of organisations outside the UK which are approved by the Registrar General. If applicant lives in a country which is not included, he will need to contact a counselling organisation in his own country. When the applicant sends his application form to the Registrar General, he will need to supply information about the organisation (ie history, experience of adoption counselling, whether officially approved) for the Registrar General's consideration.

There may be a fee for counselling outside the UK. This is a matter for the counselling organistion to determine.

4

# WHAT THE COUNSELLOR WILL RECEIVE FROM THE REGISTRAR GENERAL

Provided the Registrar General is satisfied about the body or organisation which is to provide counselling, he will send the counsellor:

i. appropriate guidance leaflets;

ii. a copy of the adopted person's application endorsed with the name of the court which made the adoption order and the number, if any, of the adoption application;

iii. the information that will supply the adopted person with his birth records, namely, his original name and that of his natural parents (this is the information that section 51 of the Adoption Act 1976 requires the Registrar General to supply). This information will be entered on a form which the applicant may use to obtain a birth certificate*;

iv. an authorisation to enable the applicant, if he wishes, to obtain from the court the name of the adoption society or local authority, if any, which took part in the adoption proceedings;

v. a form to be signed and returned to the Registrar General by the counsellor to show that counselling has taken place.

---

\* This will show the date and place of birth, the applicant's mother's name (and possibly her occupation), the informant's name and address, the date of registration and the name of the registrar. The father's name and occupation may or may not be shown.

# TOOLS FOR COUNSELLING

The counsellor may be asked about the mechanics of adoption and will therefore find it helpful to be familiar with UK adoption practice and procedures. He will also need to know what information will now be available to the adopted person from the Registrar General's records. In particular, he will need to be clear about the difference between the information which the Registrar General will provide and the additional information the adopted person will be able to obtain by buying a birth certificate for a standard fee. This difference is spelt out in the leaflet 'Information for Adopted People'. The counsellor may also find it helpful to know what information is contained in an adoption certificate which the adopted person may have and in what way this differs from a full birth certificate. Examples are reproduced at Appendix D. The format of some certificates may vary from the examples shown.

# THE ROLE OF THE COUNSELLOR

In many, perhaps most, instances the counsellor's role will be important but limited. The task is to be as helpful as possible in establishing and meeting the adopted person's need for information; and to try to help him to understand the consequences of any action he may take.

The counsellor does not have the right to withhold the basic information which will give the adopted person access to his birth records. This applies in all but the most exceptional cases where the counsellor is worried about possible consequences when the counsellor should obtain the advice of the Registrar General. Potential problems may be minimised by the use of social work skills and perhaps by contacting individuals or agencies involved, but additional counselling after the first interview will need to be by mutual agreement. The applicant will have been asked to bring with him some evidence as to his identity, eg. medical card, passport/identity card, driving licence, and this should be checked.

# RECORDS

It is important that records are kept of all interviews.

# ADOPTION CONTACT REGISTER

The Registrar General also maintains at the General Register Office an Adoption Contact Register, the purpose of which is to put adopted persons and their relatives in touch with each other if this is their stated wish. Further information about this Register for both adopted persons and their relatives is contained in leaflet ACR110 available from the Registrar General at the address on page 3. For people adopted in Scotland, a separate voluntary service is provided and information can be obtained from Birth Link, Family Care, 21 Castle Street, Edinburgh EH2 3DN, Scotland.

# REGISTERS MAINTAINED BY THE REGISTRAR GENERAL

The Registrar General is required to maintain a register recording details of all adoption orders made in England and Wales. This register, known as the Adopted Children Register, is at the General Register Office, Adoptions Section, Smedley Hydro, Trafalgar Road, Birkdale, Southport PR8 2HH, England.

When an adoption order is made, the court directs the Registrar General to have the original entry of the child's birth in the Register of Births marked with the word 'adopted'. Central records of original entries are in the custody of the Registrar General at St. Catherines House, Kingsway, London WC2, England. The details of the adoption are then recorded in an entry in the Adopted Children Register and an adoption certificate which replaces a birth certificate for an adopted person is then issued. Apart from giving the names of the adopted child and his adopters, an adoption certificate names the court which made the adoption order and the date on which it was made. A shortened form of certificate is also available which, like all short forms of birth certificate, shows only the child's name, sex and the date and place of birth, but does not contain any details of parentage. Short adoption certificates do not refer to adoption and give the country instead of district of birth, although early issues show only the country of birth.

The Index to the Adopted Children Register is open to public inspection at St. Catherines House but the method by which the entries in the Adopted Children Register are linked with those in the Register of Births is confidential and, apart from the provisions of the Adoption Act 1976, no information as to the cross-referencing may be divulged to any person except by order of the court. The effect of section 51 of the Adoption Act 1976 is to require the Registrar General to release information from these confidential records to the adopted adult so as to enable him to apply for a certified copy of the original entry of his birth in the Register of Births.

# SECTION 51 OF THE ADOPTION ACT 1976*

(1)  Subject to what follows, the Registrar General shall on an application made in the prescribed manner by an adopted person a record of whose birth is kept by the Registrar General and who has attained the age of 18 years supply to that person on payment of the prescribed fee (if any) such information as is necessary to enable that person to obtain a certified copy of the record of his birth.

(2)  On an application made in the prescribed manner by an adopted person under the age of 18 years, a record of whose birth is kept by the Registrar General and who is intending to be married in England or Wales, and on payment of the prescribed fee (if any), the Registrar General shall inform the applicant whether or not it appears from the information contained in the registers of live births or other records that the applicant and the person whom he intends to marry may be within the prohibited degrees of relationship for the purposes of the Marriage Act 1949.

(3)  Before supplying any information to an applicant under subsection (1), the Registrar General shall inform the applicant that counselling services are available to him -

(a)   if he is in England and Wales -

(i)   at the General Register Office;

(ii)   from the local authority in whose area he is living;

(iii)   where the adoption order relating to him was made in England and Wales, from the local authority in whose area the court which made the order sat; or

(iv)   from any other local authority;

(b)   if he is in Scotland -

(i)   from the regional or islands council in whose area he is living;

(ii)   where the adoption order relating to him was made in Scotland, from the council in whose area the court which made the order sat; or

(iii)   from any other regional or islands council;

---

(*As amended by Children Act 1989)

(c)  if he is in Northern Ireland -

(i)  from the Board in whose area he is living;

(ii)  where the adoption order relating to him was made in Northern Ireland, from the Board in whose area the court which made the order sat; or

(iii)  from any other Board;

(d)  if he is in the United Kingdom and his adoption was arranged by an adoption society -

(i)  approved under section 3,

(ii)  approved under section 3 of the Adoption (Scotland) Act 1978,

(iii)  registered under Article 4 of the Adoption (Northern Ireland) Order 1987,

from that society.

(4)  Where an adopted person who is in England and Wales -

(a) applies for information under -

(i)  subsection (1), or

(ii)  Article 54 of the Adoption (Northern Ireland) Order 1987, or

(b) is supplied with information under section 45 of the Adoption (Scotland) Act 1978,

it shall be the duty of the persons and bodies mentioned in subsection (5) to provide counselling for him if asked by him to do so.

(5)  The persons and bodies are -

(a) the Registrar General;

(b) any local authority falling within subsection (3)(a)(ii) to (iv);

(c) any adoption society falling within subsection (3)(d) in so far as it is acting as an adoption society in England and Wales.

(6)  If the applicant chooses to receive counselling from a person or body falling within subsection (3), the Registrar General shall send to the person or body the information to which the applicant is entitled under subsection (1).

(7)  Where a person -
(a) was adopted before 12th November 1975, and
(b) applies for information under subsection (1),
the Registrar General shall not supply the information to him unless he has
attended an interview with a counsellor arranged by a person or body from
whom counselling services are available as mentioned in subsection (3).

(8)  Where the Registrar General is prevented by subsection (7) from supplying
information to a person who is not living in the United Kingdom, he may
supply the information to any body which -
(a) the Registrar General is satisfied that it is suitable to provide counselling to
that person; and counselling to that person, and
(b) has notified the Registrar General that it is prepared to provide such
counselling.

(9)  In this section -
"a Board" means a Health and Social Services Board established under
Article 16 of the Health and Personal Social Services (Northern Ireland)
Order 1972; and
"prescribed" means prescribed by regulations made by the Registrar General..

11

# APPENDIX C

## FORM OF APPLICATION FOR ACCESS TO BIRTH RECORDS BY A PERSON ADOPTED BEFORE 12 NOVEMBER 1975

1.  I hereby apply for the information necessary to enable me to obtain a certified copy of the record of my birth. I understand that before this information is given to me, I am required to attend an interview with a counsellor.

Either  A.  I am in the United Kingdom and would prefer the interview to take place at (please put a tick in the box indicating your choice):–

    (a)  the General Register Office; ☐

    (b)  the local authority (in England or Wales), the regional or island council (in Scotland) or the Health and Social Security Board (in Northern Ireland) in whose area I am residing; ☐

    (c)  some other local authority; regional or island council or Board (Please specify which) ............................................................... ☐
.................................................................................................;

or, if known,

    (d)  the adoption society approved under section 3 of the Adoption Act 1976, Section 3 of the Adoption (Scotland) Act 1978 or registered under Article 4 of the Adoption (Northern Ireland) Order 1987 which arranged my adoption. The name and address of the approved adoption society is ........................................... ☐
.................................................................................................
.................................................................................................
.................................................................................................

Or  B.  I am living outside the United Kingdom and would prefer the interview to take place with a counsellor from ............................................................................................
(name, address and status of organisation willing to provide counselling).

I enclose that organisation's notification that it is prepared to provide such counselling.

2.  The following are the particulars of my adoption:–
Full name and surname ......................................................................................
Date of birth ......................................................................................................
Country of birth (if known) ...............................................................................
Name of adoptive father ....................................................................................
Name of adoptive mother ..................................................................................
Date of adoption (if known) ..............................................................................

3.  Declaration
I declare that to the best of my knowledge and belief I am the adopted person to whom the above particulars relate and that my adoption is recorded at entry number†
in the Adopted Children Register.

Signature:                                     Date:
Address: .......................................................................
.......................................................................
.......................................................................

---

†This number will be found in the column headed "No. of Entry" on a full certificate and in the bottom left hand corner of most short certificates.

12

# FORM OF APPLICATION FOR ACCESS TO BIRTH RECORDS BY A PERSON ADOPTED AFTER 11 NOVEMBER 1975

1.   I hereby apply for the information necessary to enable me to obtain a certified copy of the record of my birth.

2.   I understand, that if I am in the UK a counselling service is available to me. I wish/do not wish to see a counsellor. (Please delete as required, and if you have chosen to see a counsellor, tick one of the boxes in 3 below).

3.   I would like to see a counsellor at:-
   (a)  the General Register Office; ☐
   (b)  the local authority (in England or Wales), the regional or island council (in Scotland) or the Health and Social Security Board (in Northern Ireland) in whose area I am residing; ☐
   (c)  some other local authority; regional or island council or Board (Please specify which) ............................................................................................................................ ☐
   ..........................................................................................................................................;

   or, if known,

   (d)  the adoption society approved under section 3 of the Adoption Act 1976, Section 3 of the Adoption (Scotland) Act 1978 or registered under Article 4 of the Adoption (Northern Ireland) Order 1987 which arranged my adoption. The name and address of the approved adoption society is ............................................ ☐
   ..........................................................................................................................................
   ..........................................................................................................................................
   ..........................................................................................................................................

4.   The following are the particulars of my adoption:-
Full name and surname ..............................................................................................................
Date of birth ..............................................................................................................................
Country of birth (if known) .......................................................................................................
Name of adoptive father ...........................................................................................................
Name of adoptive mother ..........................................................................................................
Date of adoption (if known) .......................................................................................................

5.   Declaration

   I declare that to the best of my knowledge and belief I am the adopted person to whom the above particulars relate and that my adoption is recorded at entry number†                    in the Adopted Children Register.

   Signature:                                                          Date:
   Address:- ...............................................................................
   ...............................................................................
   ...............................................................................

---

†This number will be found in the column headed "No. of Entry" on a full certificate and in the bottom left hand corner of most short certificates.

# APPENDIX D

NB: This is a sample copy.      NB: This is a sample copy.

## CERTIFIED COPY OF AN ENTRY OF BIRTH

GIVEN AT THE GENERAL REGISTER OFFICE, LONDON.

Application Number ×××××

**REGISTRATION DISTRICT** Hendon

1964. BIRTH in the Sub-district of Finchley in the London Borough of Barnet

| No. | When and where born | Name, if any | Sex | Name and surname of father | Name, surname and maiden surname of mother | Occupation of father | Signature, description and residence of informant | When registered | Signature of registrar | Name entered after registration |
|---|---|---|---|---|---|---|---|---|---|---|
| 10 | 10 January 1964 Finchley Nursing Home Finchley | Martha Jayne | girl | | Martha SMITH Typist of 4 Elm Road Finchley | | M Smith Mother 4 Elm Road Finchley | Fourth February 1964 | F Brown Registrar | Adopted |

CERTIFIED to be a true copy of an entry in the certified copy of a Register of Births in the District above mentioned.
Given at the GENERAL REGISTER OFFICE, LONDON, under the Seal of the said Office, the Tenth day of March 1968.

J White Superintendent Registrar

This certificate is issued in pursuance of the Births and Deaths Registration Act 1953. Section 34 provides that any certified copy of an entry purporting to be sealed or stamped with the seal of the General Register Office shall be received as evidence of the birth or death to which it relates without any further or other proof of the entry, and no certified copy purporting to have been given in the said Office shall be of any force or effect unless it is sealed or stamped as aforesaid.

CAUTION:—It is an offence to falsify a certificate or to make or knowingly use a false certificate or a copy of a false certificate intending it to be accepted as genuine to the prejudice of any person, or to possess a certificate knowing it to be false without lawful authority.

*See note overleaf.

Form A502  Dd 8098353  R640159  40M  12 88  Mcr 7367781

---

## CERTIFIED COPY OF AN ENTRY IN THE RECORDS OF THE GENERAL REGISTER OFFICE

Given at the GENERAL REGISTER OFFICE

Application Number ×××××

| No. of entry | Date and country of birth of child | Name and surname of child | Sex of child | Name and surname, address and occupation of adopter or adopters | Date of adoption order and description of court by which made | Date of entry | Signature of officer deputed by Registrar General to attest the entry |
|---|---|---|---|---|---|---|---|
| 635 | First November 1962 England | Andrew Patrick Ridgway | male | Stanley Ridgway 22 Fir Tree Terrace London SW1 Planning Engineer and Jean Ridgway his wife of the same address | Twenty sixth March 1963 Chelsea Juvenile Court | Ninth April 1963 | B H Martin |

CERTIFIED copy of an entry in the Adopted Children Register maintained at the General Register Office given at the GENERAL REGISTER OFFICE, under the Seal of the said Office, the Tenth day of July 1964.

This certificate is issued pursuant to the Adoption Act 1958.

By Section 20 of the Act, a certified copy of an entry in the Adopted Children Register, if purporting to be sealed or stamped with the seal of the General Register Office, shall, without any further or other proof of the entry be received as evidence of the adoption to which it relates and, where the entry contains a record of the date and country of birth of the adopted person, such certified copy shall be received as evidence of that date and country of birth in all respects as if the copy were a certified copy of an entry in the Registers of Births.

CAUTION—It is an offence to falsify a certificate or to make or knowingly use a false certificate or a copy of a false certificate intending it to be accepted as genuine to the prejudice of any person or to possess a certificate knowing it to be false without lawful authority.

Form A50a  Dd 8272058  8106592  3M  6/91  Mcr 2325171

---

ACR 113

Prepared by Department of Health

Printed in the UK September 1991.

# Access

## to

# Birth Records

## Counselling Organisations
## Outside the United Kingdom

A NEW FRAMEWORK FOR THE CARE
AND UPBRINGING OF CHILDREN

ACR114

This leaflet is issued in connection with the introduction, on 14 October 1991, of the Children Act 1989. It gives details of counselling bodies or organisations in Australia, Canada, South Africa and New Zealand which the Registrar General for England and Wales has approved to provide adoption counselling. The information focuses on these countries since most of those adopted in the UK and now living abroad reside in one of these four countries.

Adopted people should read this leaflet in conjunction with leaflet ACR 101 "Access to Birth Records: Information for Adopted People Living Outside the UK". Counsellors should also read leaflet ACR 113 "Access to Birth Records: Notes for Counsellors". Copies are available from the Adoptions Section, The General Register Office, Office of Population Censuses and Surveys, Smedley Hydro, Trafalgar Road, Birkdale, Southport, PR8 2HH, England.

The information in this leaflet does not apply to persons whose birth records are kept by the Registrar General in Northern Ireland. Any such persons who wish to be advised about their position with regard to obtaining access to their birth record should write to:—

The Registrar General
Oxford House
49–55 Chichester Street
Belfast
Northern Ireland
BT1 4HL

Under the Adoption Act 1976, adults (at least 18 years of age) who were adopted in England or Wales can apply to the Registrar General for access to the original record of their birth. People adopted before 12 November 1975 are required to see a counsellor before they can be given access to their records. Adopted people living outside the UK have frequently been unable to exercise their right of access to their birth record because the Adoption Act made no provision for people to receive counselling except within the UK. This position is amended by provisions of the Children Act 1989 which enables people who were adopted before 12 November 1975 to take advantage of the access provisions without having to travel to the UK for a counselling interview. Statutory counselling is not required where the person was adopted in Scotland.

Anyone living in one of the countries features in this leaflet who is required to receive adoption counselling and wishes to be counselled in their own country is advised to contact the appropriate organisation. If you live in a country which is not included in this leaflet, you should contact a counselling organisation in your own country. Leaflet ACR 101 gives further details and also provides information about how to apply to the Registrar General for access to birth records.

There may be a fee for counselling outside the UK. This is a matter for the counselling organisation to determine.

A further leaflet ACR 100 "Access to Birth Records: Information for Adopted People in the UK" provides information for those who are living in the UK or who are living overseas but who intend to travel to the UK for counselling.

Each state and territory government has its own legislation regulating adoption. The Social Welfare Department in each state and territory is responsible for handling enquiries about adoption.

People seeking information about counselling services in connection with adoption are advised to contact the appropriate state or territorial offices in which they reside.

**New South Wales**
Executive Officer
Adoptions Unit
Department of Family and
 Community Services
31–39 Macquarie Street
Parramata, 2124
New South Wales
Telephone: (61) (2) 689 8111

**Australian Capital Territory**
Executive Director
Community Welfare Branch
Department of Justice and
 Community Services
PO Box 825
Canberra City
A.C.T. 2601
Telephone: (61) (6) 245 4660

**Victoria**
Officer in Charge
Intercountry Adoption Service
29 Coventry Street
South Melbourne
Victoria, 3205
Telephone: (61) (3) 693 3888

**Tasmania**
Officer in Charge
Adoptions Branch
Department of Community Services
GPO Box 125B
Hobart 7001
Tasmania

3

**Queensland**

Manager
Adoptions Section
Department of Family Services
  and Aboriginal and
· Islander Affairs
GPO Box 806
Brisbane QLD
4011
Telephone: (61) (70) 224 2545

**Northern Territory**

The Co-ordinator
Adoption and Substitute Care
Department of Health and
  Community Services
PO Box 405096
Casuarina
NT 0811
Telephone: (61) (89) 227 472

**Western Australia**

Department for Community
  Services
189 Royal Street
East Perth
WA 6004
Telephone: (61) (9) 222 2555

**South Australia**

Operations Manager
Adoption Services
Family and Community Services
PO Box 10037
Gouger Street
Adelaide 5000
South Australia

# NEW ZEALAND

Counselling of adopted people seeking information about their birth records is carried out by the Department of Social Welfare, or by a voluntary agency or independent counsellor approved by the Department.

Enquiries in the first instance should be made to the address given below.

The Director General
Department of Social Welfare
Head Office
Private Bag 21, Postal Centre
Wellington 1
Telephone: (04) 727 666

# SOUTH AFRICA

The Department of Health Services and Welfare has responsibility for adoption. The provision of counselling Services can be carried out by Welfare Organisations or independent social workers approved by the Department.

An adopted person from the United Kingdom now residing in South Africa should contact the Department of Health Services and Welfare in the first instance.

The Head of the Department
Department of Health Services
  and Welfare: Administration
House of Assembly
Private Bag X730
Pretoria
0001

# CANADA

Responsibility for adoption matters rests with each province and territory.

People seeking information about counselling services in connection with adoption are advised to contact the appropriate office in the province or territory in which they reside.

**British Columbia**
Manager, Adoption Program
Family and Children's Services
Ministry of Social Services
  and Housing
Parliament Buildings
Victoria
British Columbia
V8W 3A2
Telephone: (604) 387 7059

**Alberta**
Program Supervisor
Adoption Services
Department of Social Services
12th Floor, Seventh Street Plaza
10030–107th Street
Edmonton
Alberta
T5J 3E4
Telephone: (403) 422 0178

**Saskatchewan**

Program Manager
Adoption Services
Family Support Division
Department of Social Services
12th Floor, 1920 Broad Street
Regina
Saskatchewan
S4P 3V7
Telephone: (306) 787 5698

**Manitoba**

Adoption Co-ordinator
Adoptions and Field Services
Department of
 Community Services
114 Garry Street
Winnipeg
Manitoba
R3C 1G1
Telephone: (204) 945 6955

**Ontario**

Adoption Policy and
 Program Planning
Children's Services Branch
Ministry of Community and
 Social Services
2 Bloor Street West
24th Floor
Toronto
Ontario
M7A 1E9
Telephone: (416) 327 4724

**Quebec**

Directeur
Secrétariat à l'adoption
 internationale
3700 rue Berri, 4 ième étage
Montréal (Quebec)
H2L 4G9
Telephone: (514) 873 5226

**New Brunswick**

Program Consultant for
 Adoption Service
Department of Health and
 Community Services
PO Box 5100
Fredericton
New Brunswick
E3B 5G8
Telephone: (506) 453 3830

**Nova Scotia**

Co-ordinator, Children in Care
Family and Children's Services
Department of Social Services
PO Box 696
Halifax
Nova Scotia
B3J 2T7
Telephone: (902) 424 3205

**Prince Edward Island**

Co-ordinator, Children in Care
Department of Health and
  Social Services
PO Box 2000
Charlottetown
Prince Edward Island
C1A 7N8
Telephone: (902) 368 4931/2

**Newfoundland**

Director of Child Welfare Services
Department of Social Services
3rd Floor, West Block
Confederation Building
PO Box 4750
St. John's
Newfoundland
A1C 5T7
Telephone: (709) 729 2667

**Northwest Territories**

Program Officer, Child Welfare
Family and Children's Services
Department of Social Services
Government of the N.W.T.
Yellowknife
N.W.T.
X1A 2L9
Telephone: (403) 873 7943

**Yukon Territory**

Placement and Support
  Services Supervisor
Department of Health and
  Human Resources
PO Box 2703, H-10, Suite 201
Royal Bank Building
Whitehorse
Yukon Territory
Y1A 2C6
Telephone: (403) 667 3002

ACR 114
Prepared by Department of Health
Printed in the UK September 1991